Chicken Soup with Chopsticks

A Paper Spider Production
Ottawa, Canada

Chicken Soup

with

Chopsticks

A Jew's Struggle
for Truth
in an Interfaith Relationship

by Jack Botwinik

Attention corporations, associations, and organizations: Enjoy 40% off and use our books as fund-raisers, premiums, or gifts. Phone *Paper Spider* at 1-888-BOOKS-88 or 613-321-9850 to arrange.

For school libraries and charitable organizations: Learn more about our *Special Donations Program* and *Free Books for School Libraries Program* on our web site at

http://www.PaperSpider.Net/about/

Printed in the United States of America.

Library and Archives Canada Cataloguing in Publication

Botwinik, Jack, 1965–
        Chicken soup with chopsticks : a Jew's struggle for truth in an interfaith relationship / by Jack Botwinik.

Includes bibliographical references.
Also available in electronic format.
ISBN 0-9732523-0-8 (bound)—ISBN 0-9732523-1-6 (pbk.)

    1. Botwinik, Jack, 1965- 2. Interfaith marriage. 3. Judaism. I. Title.
HQ1031.B769 2005   306.84'3'092   C2004-904905-4

Dedication

To all of us who struggle with

God.

Epigraph

There's a special time each year when Jews erect small shelters, called sukkahs, just outside their homes. Each day for a week we sit in this shelter to eat, talk, read, sing, and enjoy life. We invite guests.

Sometimes we spend time in the sukkah of a neighbour or a total stranger. The roof is flimsy, consisting of branches and leaves. On a clear night, one can see through to the stars. The sukkah is beautifully decorated to reflect this joyous time. At night, if it's not raining, people sleep in it. The Jewish religion instructs us to step out of our secure houses and live in such a temporary dwelling for an entire week every year. We are called upon to remember, through total immersion in the experience, that our "houses" (our bodies, our material possessions) are fragile and temporary, and that our lives are at the mercy of our Creator.

"Jack Botwinik has made a wonderfully inspiring contribution to the literature of Jewish spiritual autobiography. I am full of admiration for his insights, clear thinking, and dedication to Truth. His book is a pleasure to read — concise, humble, entirely authentic."

— David Klinghoffer,
Author of The Discovery of God:
Abraham and the Birth of Monotheism

"I simply could not put it down. Your story is not only inspiring and thought-provoking but is a great read: funny, poignant, suspenseful, informative...In short, everything that a good book should be."

— Maria R. Bloshteyn, Ph.D.

"This is a sensitive account of a spiritual odyssey. In a moving and clear style, Botwinik shares a psychological tale of many seekers, with its struggles, perseverance, and blessings."

— Leah Cohen, Cataloguer,
Library and Archives Canada

Contents

Photos

Preface

"What are we waiting for?" my girlfriend asked, buoyant yet somewhat confused as we sat cross-legged on the carpet, facing each other in the privacy of my apartment. For weeks we had been talking about the prospect of getting married. For weeks we had been affirming our compatibility, corroborating our common values, reaffirming that we would take the best of each of our worlds and build a happy, culturally-rich family.

She was, essentially, proposing to me! I was tempted to say *yes*. I was twenty-nine and wanted desperately to settle down and start a family. It was a strong value that my parents and older siblings had ingrained in me.

I held back. I was not supposed to marry a gentile, I thought. To do so would be a shocking betrayal of my family, my ancestors, my tradition.

It would sound racist if I told her that. It would sound racist not only to her, but to me as well.

I was cognizant that I was the product of 3,300 years of Jewish history. I was sensitive to the loss of one-third of my people in the Holocaust and to the assimilation that now threatened us. Despite this, and despite my parents' repeated threat to cut off all contact with me, and the disapproval I feared from the broader Jewish community, I was determined to keep my options open.

The issue was not about love for someone from a different background versus loyalty to my own kind. The issue was very emotional, but it was not *about* emotions. The issue, ultimately, was about what would be the right thing to do. I was an independent thinker, not one to blindly follow the views of my community. That is another strong value that I acquired from my family.

Chicken Soup with Chopsticks is the story[1] of my encounter with a wonderful Chinese woman and how the budding relationship catapulted us on a spiritual journey into the unknown, culminating in our discovery and adoption of a seemingly bizarre, yet beautiful and meaningful way of life. It is a tale of inner struggle, questioning, hope, and the power of love; a story of breaking and repairing family ties and challenging community norms. Underpinning all this is a desperate and urgent quest for Truth.

Many books have been written about the often-impetuous meeting of faiths, particularly between Jews and Christians. Some warn of the dire consequences of intermarriage. Others offer practical guidance and reassurance for fostering harmonious family relationships. A few books focus on interdating, which is recognized as a serious problem within Jewish communities as it is a stepping-stone to intermarriage and further assimilation. This story about interdating unfolds differently.

Is it wrong for a Jew to date a gentile? Thousands of Jews struggle with this question every day. I was one of them.

---

1. Some names have been altered to protect the privacy of people mentioned in the story.

Acknowledgements

I wish to express my heartfelt gratitude to the following individuals for their time and commitment in reviewing my manuscript at various stages in its development, and offering their frank and constructive criticism: Helen Song and Kit Barham, Judith Barrington, Rabbi Mordechai Becher, Dr. Maria R. Bloshteyn, Rabbi Dr. Reuven P. Bulka, Leah Cohen, Jane Enkin and Rabbi Justin Lewis, Farla Klaiman, Diane Parkin, Michael Schaub, Palbinder Shergill, Adele Sidney, Rabbi Michael Skobac, Rabbi Reuven Tradburks, and Matt Wexler.

Each, in his or her way, helped enhance the quality of this book.

I also thank my dear parents, and my brothers, Leybl and Sender, and sister-in-law, Naomi, for their helpful suggestions, their love and support, and their interest in seeing this project to fruition.

I am forever indebted to my wife, Bina Ester, for her constant support and encouragement, her invaluable assistance, and her selflessness.

Above all, I thank God for His countless blessings, including having introduced me to my wife. Had I not met her, this book would not have been written.

1

Embarking on an Adventure

One day in seven, for twenty-five hours, my wife and I do not operate any electrical equipment. We don't drive, answer our phone, use an elevator, watch television, listen to the radio, or switch lights on or off. If it's cold, we don't adjust the thermostat. We don't boil water, knead, or cook. Nor do we write, tear paper, or discuss personal finances. My wife and I are observant Jews. Our religion teaches that this is what the Creator commands. It's part of our prescribed role. And the sole reason God wants this from us is for our benefit and that of humankind.

Does God Care if I Marry a Gentile?

*E*ven as I started dating a Chinese girl, I knew I was embarking on a remarkable adventure. I just had no idea where and how far the adventure would take me. The more events unfolded, the more I realized that my view of the world and how I lived in it were being profoundly and permanently altered.

Relationships often end because of boredom, infidelity, lack of mutual attraction, diverging interests, selfishness, or countless other "valid" reasons. I felt that if my relationship with this Asian girl were to end, the reason would be nobler, one, in fact, that I had been grappling with for years and was unable to resolve: Is it wrong for a Jew to date and marry a gentile?

The arguments were basically as follows: Suppose I met a girl who is beautiful in my eyes, is of good character, and has the same values as I—in other words, someone who is decent, kind, charitable, environmentally concerned, someone who has a strong love of life, honours her parents, and so on—why should I not marry her?

Then again, if she were Christian, there would be an emotional shadow hovering over our relationship, a shadow cast by centuries of persecution of Jews, expulsions, and pogroms; the historical experience of enforced conversions, such as during the Crusades, with countless Jews choosing to give up their lives rather than bow down to another deity; and more recently, the Holocaust and the supporting role of those Christians who kept silent while knowing that millions of Jews were being systematically slaughtered—all of this in the name of "Christ." And residual feelings of anti-Semitism might, perhaps unknowingly, linger in her family.

If the girl I met were Muslim, there would be the issue of the protracted Middle East conflict and the seemingly irreconcilable hatred between Arabs[2] and Jews.

---

2. Although only a minority of Muslims are Arabs, the distinction did not figure prominently in my mind.

If she were Hindu or Buddhist, her religion would be so foreign to me, with its many gods and rituals of worship, that I might never feel totally comfortable even though I might become familiar with the religion.

Thus, if I *were* to date a non-Jewish girl, the best option, it seemed, would be to find an atheist, particularly one whose family would tolerate intermarriage.

A close friend dated such a girl. The relationship went smoothly for a few years. As it turned out, they broke up for other reasons. Soon he found a Christian girl, and they went to church on Sundays and synagogue on Saturdays. Eventually she adopted Reform Judaism.[3] Another close friend found a Catholic girl who eventually converted to Orthodox Judaism after claiming to discover truth and beauty in the religion. He himself was inspired to grow in his Jewish knowledge and became Orthodox as well, a turn of events that baffled me. They were married soon after.

So, I surmised, anything could happen. If the problem with marrying a gentile was that my religion prohibited inter-marriage, why should that bother me? Perhaps not everything in Judaism made sense, and as an intelligent and thinking individual I could take from my heritage what I felt was meaningful and disregard the rest. Besides, to the extent that

---

3. There are three main denominations of Judaism in North America: Orthodox, Conservative, and Reform. Orthodox Judaism is the strictest in adherence to observance. Reform Judaism is the most liberal in interpretation of the Hebrew Bible and observance of its laws. Conservative Judaism lies between the two. A fourth denomination, Reconstructionism, has emerged in the past several decades.

Judaism is a beautiful and worthwhile religion, why would she not *want* to convert?

I had eleven years of formal Jewish education: the primary and secondary schools that I attended were Jewish. We studied Jewish history, Jewish traditions, Jewish languages (Hebrew and Yiddish), Jewish literature and culture, as well as the *Torah*. We celebrated the holidays. Because it was a secular school system, most of the students did not observe the kosher dietary laws or keep *Shabbos*. Girls and boys wore jeans; flirting was widespread; and the caressing and kissing in the open made me uneasy, as if I were intruding on other people's private affairs. It was a liberal school system where Jewish culture and tradition, love of the State of Israel, and Jewish pride were stressed, but belief in God was not. That the Hebrew Bible is the true, immutable word of God was presented as an opinion and generally not taken seriously by students or faculty.

In high school we dreamed of becoming doctors, lawyers, or engineers, or perhaps politicians or architects. I was less pragmatically minded. I wanted to become a theoretical physicist and dreamed of unravelling the mystery of the origin of the universe. There was the perception that the Judaic studies component would not assist us in meeting our career goals. Judaism had its place: Israel, the Holocaust, Jewish culture, Jewish wisdom, and Jewish literature linked us to our ancestors, and identified us as a distinct people. However, the Judaic subjects were considered less important than mathematics or world history. Like many of my peers, I often wondered of what use all this Jewish immersion would be in the long run.

Although we lived in a heavily Jewish area of Montreal, the broader society was predominantly Catholic. Not surprisingly, the question of intermarriage sometimes surfaced, inside and outside the classroom. I sensed that intermarriage, though not condemned, was frowned upon by the school administration.

The possibility that *God Himself*[4] does not want a Jew to marry a gentile is not something I recall being taught explicitly. This may be because, even though I believed in God in my own nebulous way, I didn't take seriously the proposition that God authored the Torah. For one thing, I considered many claims in the Torah absurd: that the world is less than 6,000 years old, that Noah lived more than 900 years and built an ark to house the planet's animals, and that a sea parted miraculously to enable the Hebrews to escape their Egyptian pursuers. As far as I was concerned, these were stories with possible moral messages but not actual facts. *If the Bible were true, then the theory of evolution, and much of science, must be wrong.* In a world where humans went to the moon, performed brain surgery, and saw and talked to people on the other side of the planet, I had far more trust in what modern science presumed than in what the Bible stated.

Furthermore, I believed that religion was a crutch that societies invented to help them cope with life's uncertainties and challenges. Nor could I fathom that of all the different

4. According to Jewish teachings, God has both female and male attributes. For simplicity, this narrative follows the convention of using the masculine pronoun in reference to God.

religions in the world, it just so happened that Judaism — *my* religion — was "the Truth."

But the issue of intermarriage became more relevant in college. There I was exposed to many gentile women while my interest in having a girlfriend intensified. I frequented the Jewish students' association. One time it organized an interesting event on intermarriage, where participants were invited to choose sides and the two teams debated. Attendance was overflowing and the evening turned out to be very lively. I found myself shifting position several times during the debate, only to end up on the fence.

"I think love and mutual commitment are the two most important things in a relationship," said one student. "Being Jewish is not that important. Just because you're Jewish doesn't mean you're better or part of an elite group."

"What about Jewish continuity?" argued another. "Does four thousand years of a civilization that has given the world the Bible, humane values, a sophisticated legal system, and so much more, mean nothing to us? Do we want to be the generation that breaks that chain? I wouldn't want to be responsible for that. I wouldn't be able to live with myself."

"Why must we let the past dictate our lives and limit our choices? We all take from our heritage what we find relevant and meaningful, and incorporate other beautiful and positive values that come our way. I believe in changing, evolving, growing."

"Wake up, guys!" chimed someone else. "Hitler tried to exterminate our people, and almost succeeded. Now we are doing it to ourselves!"

"Hitler was a madman," retorted another student. "He wanted to annihilate everyone, not just Jews. I am a Canadian. I am a woman. I am a law student. I also happen to be Jewish. So what? I shouldn't marry an American just because I am a proud Canadian? If most people hate lawyers, I should therefore only date lawyers?"

And so the exchanges went. Although both sides made good points, one of the boldest arguments against intermarriage that surfaced was, "God said so." That, to me, sounded arrogant and narrow-minded and, if anything, served to discredit the anti-intermarriage position.

Ideological Immersion

My relationship with Judaism was greatly influenced by my deep connection to the Yiddish language and culture. Yiddish was, until the Holocaust, the most commonly spoken language among European Jews. Most post-Holocaust European immigrants to North America chose to speak to their children and grandchildren in broken English rather than their native tongue. There was little desire to transmit the thousand-year-old language to future generations. It is as if they wanted to keep the treasures of Yiddish for themselves, while protecting their children from the burden of learning a foreign and "archaic" language.

An entire generation of *Ashkenazi* Jews grew up with Yiddish spoken at home around them, but not *to* them. This was particularly the case in Montreal, where most young Jews were children or grandchildren of immigrants. By adulthood they understood Yiddish but had trouble speaking it. Many recollected that Yiddish felt like a secret language, spoken between parents when they didn't want the children to understand.

Not surprisingly, many of my peers developed a negative attitude, if not utter disdain, toward the language. Yiddish was associated with the Old World, the ghettos, the anti-Semitism of Eastern Europe. It was useless at best, and regressive at worst. Perhaps the language also sounded too much like German.

My father went against the grain and fought what he called "discrimination" against the language, the perceived attempt by many within the Jewish cultural elite to hasten its demise. He published a magazine in which, through story, song, art, and humour, he sought to promote Yiddish as a living, breathing language, especially among youth. He also incessantly berated the leaders of Jewish schools, synagogues, Jewish cultural establishments, and institutions for deliberately omitting the use of the language in their events, literature, communiqués, and so on. Whether through sending letters to the editor, handing out leaflets near the entrances to Jewish literary events, or refusing to attend funeral services of native Yiddish speakers when the eulogies were to be delivered solely in English, my father sought to press his case.

My older siblings and I were recruited in the campaign. Over a number of years, particularly during high school and college, I felt that we were more than a family: we were an ideological movement. My father tried to impress upon me the belief that Yiddish was an important means of stemming the rapid slide to assimilation that was occurring in Jewish communities the world over, the effects of which were evident in the rise of interdating, intermarriage, drug use, promiscuity, family breakdown, and all the ills of secular society. Yiddish was the natural antidote: an immediate and powerful link to the idealized pre-Holocaust world of Eastern Europe where Jewish culture flourished and healthy ideals and values guided human behaviour. (Indeed, in Yiddish the very word for "a human being"—a *mentsh*—reflects these positive humanistic values and has seeped into the diction of English-speaking Jews and a fair number of non-Jews too.)

Religion wasn't sufficient. Language, because we use it and think in it all the time, is a very effective means of identifying with a people and its experiences. Many Jews, my father would say, were campaigning to promote the Hebrew language, others were fighting for the religion, still others were activists for Zionist ideals—all worthy causes that prevented Hitler from achieving a posthumous victory of obliterating Judaism. But no one—or hardly anyone—was doing anything to stop the rapid decline of the Yiddish language. The Botwiniks were the mavericks, standing out in the secular Jewish community, ridiculed by some, admired by others, and not afraid to speak out for a noble and righteous cause.

During these formative years, I vacillated between feeling proud to be part of a Yiddishist family and harbouring ambivalence, both with respect to the mission and its prospect for success. Nonetheless, my father inculcated within me the following ideals: pride in my heritage; a disdain for following popular trends without independent critical assessment; and the virtue of working diligently and persistently for an idealistic cause.

Quest for a Life Partner

In this strong Jewish cultural environment in which I was raised, I was expected to marry one of my people. Not to do so would be a shocking betrayal of my family. The prohibition against intermarriage was so ingrained that it was hardly an appropriate subject to bring up for a family discussion.

Under the caring and watchful eyes of my parents while I lived at home in the quiet, middle-class suburb of Côte Saint-Luc, I dated many Jewish women and found the vast majority of them materialistic. They didn't seem to harbour the strong family values, desire to have children, and appreciation of culture and language that were particularly pronounced in my family. It was especially important that I find a girl who didn't blindly follow the ways of the masses, viewed life positively, respected her Jewish heritage, and would be supportive of my speaking Yiddish with our children. Was this too much to ask? Apparently, in the assimilating Jewish environs in which I grew up, it was. I really was not brought up to appreciate the virtues of a girl whose focus was on the kind of car I drove, what my father did for a living, or how often I vacationed in Florida.

Deep down, I wanted to marry someone spiritual. Notwithstanding problems with incompatible ethnic associations, if she were Christian she should be a devout Christian; if Muslim, a religious Muslim. Better yet, she could be an environmentalist or perhaps dedicated to the cause of the homeless. Basically, I longed to meet a woman who was focused on making the world a better place. I was dedicated to being a good person, and I sought a compatible soul mate who would appreciate this more than how much money I made.

One time I did meet a woman with whom I really connected. She was Jewish and religious. After dating for a month or two, she initiated our break-up. Her family was not content with my level of religious observance or that of my family.

Whereas my siblings sought only Jewish spouses, I kept my options open. I was not convinced of the necessity to restrict my search for a mate to those of my religion, especially as we constituted a tiny minority (a fraction of one percent) of the human population. Moreover, I encountered females, from various religions and backgrounds, who were extremely nice, good-natured, and attractive. My motto about intermarriage, as in other areas of life, was "I'll cross that bridge when I come to it."

Sino-Attraction

In the summer of 1994, three years after I left my parents' home in Montreal and was living on my own in Toronto, I met Belinda. I was twenty-nine; she was twenty-five. We quickly became friends.

"Would you like to see my snake?" Belinda asked, as I dropped her off in front of her building.

My heart pounded and raced.

"Okay," I heard myself saying. I knew that sooner or later she would show me her pet. I hadn't reckoned it would be *so* soon.

Belinda ran inside and returned shortly with a tiny corn snake tucked into her sleeve. Once in the car, she let me hold it. It was the first time I had held a snake. Instinctively, I applied my peripheral vision to the clammy, slender creature in my palm, imagining it was some inanimate object.

Belinda reached for my other hand. "What do you think about our relationship?" she asked.

It was the first time we had held hands. Thoughts of the biblical symbolism of the serpent and the fact that she was Chinese pulsated through my mind. At the same time, I was taken aback by her forthrightness. It was only our second date.

I took a slow, deep breath.

"As you know, Belinda, I'm marriage-minded. You told me you were too. But, I'm not interested in just getting married, having children, and leading a *normal* life. That's the *minimum* of what I would expect. I want to reach for the moon, grow together with a life-long partner, embark on an adventure with this person that would make a difference in the world."

The snake began to slither its way up my sleeve, and I pleaded for help. I don't recall anything else we talked about that evening.

❧

When I met Belinda, I had little interest in religious Judaism. I was unaware of its unique spiritual treasures and their relevance to today's world. In fact, like many of my peers, I had an affinity for secular Jewish culture, and that is where it stopped.

My father was raised in an observant family. He fled his native Poland on the eve of the Second World War. His entire family was murdered in the Holocaust, and he became a "worldly" Jew and Yiddishist. My mother, an Italian Jew, was raised with little knowledge and practice of Judaism. She always believed in God, however, and has stood firmly committed to whatever Jewish observances she was raised with.

In the world of postmodernism, where the whole idea of Truth with a capital T has fallen into disrepute among many intellectuals, I was not disposed to think differently. I did not particularly believe that there must be a Truth, but I did not rule it out either. Initially, my concern was not with intellectual truth (Is Jesus the son of God? Did God author the Bible?), as much as with a practical formula for improving the world. The formula had to be grounded in reality, or it would not work. Perhaps there were multiple formulas, and I was looking for the one that most suited *me*.

In college and university I took courses in political philosophy and became interested in Marxism, Platonism, socialism, humanism, feminism, and any other "ism" that was popular in academia. I wondered if any of them was the key to fixing the world and ushering in a utopia. I delved into the teachings of Christianity and Buddhism. I traveled to the Arctic for a month, hoping to taste native spirituality. I joined the army and sought, but did not find, patriotic pride. I spent two summers in Israel working on a kibbutz and interviewing the *vatikim*, or elders, those idealists who left the relative comfort of their European homes in the '30s and '40s to go to a harsh and barren land and pioneer a new experiment in socialism. At one point I seriously considered moving to a kibbutz and dedicating my life to the principle "from each according to his ability, to each according to his need." Later, when I moved to Toronto, I toyed with New Age ideas and started frequenting an ashram.

Belinda lived in a very different reality. Her upbringing was not politically and ideologically charged like mine. She was much more focused on academic achievement and team sports than on philosophy and the need to change the world. She grew up in a touristy section of the Kowloon peninsula, just off Hong Kong Island, a cosmopolitan area teeming with hotels, shops, temples, markets, and restaurants; a unique blend of Eastern and Western culture. There were remnants of Buddhist practice in her home. Her grandmother, during the years she shared the cramped seventh-floor flat with Belinda's family, maintained an altar with burning incense, and there were always a few oranges laid out for the gods. Belinda recalls visiting a Buddhist Temple during Chinese New Year and hating it because of the crowd and commotion. Each year the family and numerous relatives would assemble, rent a tour bus, and drive to a hilly cemetery. After exiting the vehicle, they would trek up the steep slope in the chilly winter air, venerate their ancestors, and leave flowers or food behind as gifts. Belinda enjoyed these gatherings and hikes with her relatives. But the reasons behind the worship rituals were never explained to her. From her perspective, they just happened to be part of an ever-changing tradition. They were to be performed to please the elders, who considered such practices important.

Belinda was sent to a Catholic primary school because it had a good reputation academically. She recalls a discouraging experience with her religion teacher when she was eight. The teacher was unable to provide logically satisfying responses to many of her questions. She concluded that he plucked answers out of thin air and that the stories about the Hebrews, Egypt, and the Red Sea were fabricated. She formed an impression that all religions are just hoaxes. Before she came to Canada, at the age of seventeen, Belinda didn't know that Jesus was Jewish or that Jews still existed. She figured the Jews must have long ago disappeared like the Greeks, Romans, Babylonians, and other ancient peoples.

In her early twenties Belinda started to wonder about the real meaning of life. She had been approached many times in malls by Christian evangelists, and invited to attend church services or free Bible classes; she consistently declined. Then, when she was twenty-five, a few weeks before I met her, she acceded. She figured she had nothing to lose.

After attending a few of these classes and reading the Bible (which they gave her as a gift) on her own, Belinda inquired if I would be interested in joining her.

"Sure," I said composedly, as my mouth suddenly became dry. She was looking for God. I felt I needed to show my support, notwithstanding my ethnic biases and strong sentiments against Christian dogma.

"Great! The next session is at Helen's — she's one of the members. She invited me for dinner on Tuesday at six-thirty. That's in three weeks. I just need to find out her address and confirm that I can invite you along. Although I'm sure she won't mind."

Not only will she not mind, I thought, she will probably be *ecstatic*, especially once she finds out I'm Jewish.

I feared Belinda was being indoctrinated in ideas I couldn't accept, such as "turning the other cheek," that we are all innate sinners, and that we are damned to the fires of hell unless we accept Jesus as our god and saviour. Moreover, although I was cognizant that "born-again" Christians were generally sensitive and good-natured people (such as one particular college friend I had; I never passed an opportunity to engage him in conversation about his beliefs), I also knew that for centuries the Catholic Church had promulgated hatred of Jews and associated Jews with the devil.

I recalled a documentary I had seen as a child, in which Galileo tries to defend himself against accusations of heresy by inviting the heads of the Church to peer through his telescope. The latter emphatically refuse, stating that there is no point in doing so as their theology informs them that the earth is at the centre of the universe. Despite repeated pleading from Galileo, they stubbornly refuse to be challenged by any evidence to the contrary. Their reasoning is that if, by looking through Galileo's invention, they were to observe that the earth was *not* at the centre of the universe, then it would mean one of two things: trickery or the work of Satan.

I refused to emulate the manner of those Church leaders by drawing on pre-conceived notions to rationalize not attending a free Bible class. I prided myself on being open-minded and was willing to face ideas with which I didn't necessarily agree or feel comfortable — especially if I could challenge them in front of Belinda!

As it turned out, Belinda invited me at a point when she was getting increasingly frustrated with that Bible study group. On more than one occasion she was rebuked for her questions. Very soon — before I was scheduled to go with her — she dropped out of the church, and I breathed a deep sigh of relief.

⚘

Apart from Belinda's nascent interest in discovering ultimate Truth (which stemmed from a longing to know God and connect to Him), I was drawn to her because Chinese was exotic and interesting. Also, different languages and cultures had always intrigued me. I grew up speaking Yiddish and Italian at home while living in a French-speaking province (Quebec), which itself was nestled within a predominantly English-speaking country, Canada.

Belinda and I began to explore different religions together, and we frequently talked about spiritual matters. We also talked about Disney, travel, computers, and Indian food. We were amazed at how much we had in common. Like typical romantic couples, we spent most of our free time with each other, sometimes engaging in juvenile activities. One of our favourite pastimes was to go to parks and look for trees to climb. Once we played an entire game of Chinese checkers seated high up on tree branches, with a bag of snacks hanging beside us.

I knew that when my parents found out about my latest girlfriend they would vehemently oppose the relationship unless, perhaps, Belinda were to convert to Judaism. I feared being ostracized by my immediate family. Perhaps on a deeper level, I feared cutting *myself* off from my ethnic roots. As painful as these thoughts were, they did not deter me from pursuing the course on which I had already embarked.

❦ Safe Haven

While most countries in the world closed their borders or had severely restrictive quotas for Jewish refugees fleeing the fire and ashes of the Holocaust, all the faculty and students of the renowned *Mir Yeshiva* of Poland found safe haven in Shanghai, China. There, they formed a community and were allowed to study and worship freely. In a few short years, they produced many important scholarly works. By 1945, the entire Jewish community in Shanghai numbered 30,000. After the war, all the rabbis and students of the yeshiva left China and founded the Mir Yeshiva in New York as well as the Mir Yeshiva in Jerusalem.

2

Pushing the Limits

*T*he next time we held hands — after the encounter with the snake — was in a museum. The last section of the museum, a bat cave exhibit, was dark. On the pretence that my night vision was poor, I asked Belinda if she wouldn't mind taking my hand and guiding me. On exiting the exhibit, we were still holding hands as we made our way out to the underground train. We walked in silence. The "physical" part of the relationship had arrived. *The third date. Not too soon, not too late.* It seemed to be a sign of a healthy relationship.

But just as I was enjoying these comfortable thoughts, panic gripped me. What if someone I knew happened to see us? How quickly would word spread that Jack Botwinik was dating a gentile girl? Were she not Asian, people in the community would assume that I was dating somebody Jewish and would be happy for me. *But a Jewish Chinese person?* I had never met one or heard of such a thing. I knew I was placing myself in a precarious situation wherein I could be talked about, perhaps ridiculed. It might cause many people to be upset and disappointed in me. Worst of all, I feared that my family would soon find out. Montreal was not far from Toronto and news traveled easily between the two Jewish communities. This would lead to a family crisis.

I thought of my mother. I remembered how she would frequently relate to us the story of how her mother's life had been shortened as a result of one of my uncles in Italy marrying a Catholic woman. A tragedy! I had heard that intermarriage was considered such a terrible sin that, traditionally, Jewish parents would do everything possible to break up the relationship and prevent the marriage. If in the end they failed, they would tear their clothes, cover all the mirrors in the house, sit on the floor, and mourn the "death" of their child. I would be considered a traitor to my family, to my people, to my ancestors.

My parents were proud Jews. Disgracing their names, I assumed, would affect their health, which is the last thing in the world I wanted to do. I began to question my motivation behind dating a Chinese woman. Was it rebellion? Anger? Getting back at my parents for all those years of being forced to go to a Jewish school and attend long and boring synagogue services on the High Holidays? When someone does something unusual, it can be an indication that he or she seeks attention, honour, or fame. Was I yearning for these things?

Yet, as all these thoughts passed through my mind, I knew that the painful alternative was to end the relationship with Belinda. How could I explain to her that I wasn't supposed to be holding her hand because she was not Jewish? What would she think of me? What would I think of *myself*? I had dated so many women in my life, and finally I had met someone who seemed to be perfect for me.

At the first opportunity I took Belinda to a restaurant where Jewish-style food was served. I wanted to know if she liked, or was at least amenable to, matzo ball soup, gefilte fish, and bagels and lox. I thought that if she could fit in with the Ashkenazi Jewish culture, it would be important to my family.

When I arrived home from the restaurant, I continued to revel in how fabulous our dates had been and wondered whether — or how — I should tell my parents about Belinda. I crafted a letter, one copy addressed to my parents in Montreal and the other to my brother in Philadelphia, with whom I enjoyed a close relationship. I wrote that I had met a very nice Chinese girl who was attractive, intelligent, kind, charitable, marriage-minded, wanted to have kids, and liked Jewish food. So as not to risk giving my parents a heart attack, I wrote in a way that didn't create an impression that I had "fallen in love" and become irrevocably attached to her. I indicated that a rational choice was before me: not see her again or continue to do so, as there was always the possibility that she might eventually want to become Jewish. I argued the merits of getting to know her better, and, like a good son and younger brother, solicited their advice.

No sooner did my brother receive my letter than he called and posed a string of questions about Belinda, without suggesting whether I should continue or break off the relationship. I respected that tremendously. He asked whether I had told my parents. The letter to them was sealed, stamped, and ready to be mailed the next day. I hated the idea of being secretive, but during my discussions with my brother and sister-in-law I realized that it would be wise not to inform my parents. If things didn't work out in the end, they would be saved needless aggravation and anxiety by not knowing. If they were to find out by accident, I could simply downplay the seriousness of the relationship. I needed time to think, to read up on intermarriage, to figure things out.

The next time I saw Belinda, I told her (being careful not to frighten her) a little about my family and the potential consequences of our dating. My goal was to prepare her for the worst, and not hide things from her any more than necessary. My discourse was met with a puzzled look, more because of my edgy delivery than because of the content. Belinda was unable to relate to what I was saying.

Over the next six months, as I continued dating Belinda, I immersed myself in reading and intensive contemplation of the importance of religion, particularly Judaism. This culminated in an essay I wrote to clarify for myself, and to share with Belinda, exactly why Judaism was important to me. Here are excerpts from that essay.

> Judaism is important because religion is important. Religion comforts us in times of crisis and despair. It

also honours and celebrates life's ordinary moments. Religion lifts us up when we are down, and when we are joyful it lifts us higher.

Judaism is the oldest monotheistic religion, out of which Christianity and Islam emerged. Though not a proselytizing religion, Judaism assumes its ancient role of being a "light unto the nations." The Jewish people have a historical mission to make the world better by committing themselves to high standards of ethical behaviour and being a role model for others who wish to do the same.

Through generation after generation of being victim to persecutions, expulsions, and attempts at conversion, the Jews, always a minority, have miraculously survived. Because of their steadfast refusal to endorse the beliefs of the pagans, of Christianity, or of Islam — even on penalty of death — the Jewish people survived while many other civilizations, far more mighty and populous, vanished from the earth...

To survive as a people, the Jews did not rely on arms or on their numbers or solely on the love of their religion: they were able to overcome the powerful forces of oppression and assimilation because they placed a high priority on learning and on transmitting Jewish knowledge, Jewish wisdom, Jewish ritual, and Jewish traditions to their children and grandchildren.

Having lived through such a long history of oppression, the Jews are a remarkably strong-willed and forward-looking people. They have demonstrated themselves to be peace loving, focused, and sensitive to injustice.

The Jews are independent thinkers and actors. As a consequence, whenever they were allowed to participate in society, they made outstanding, original contributions — far out of proportion to their number — in science, philosophy, art, business, and other secular fields.

I grew up with Judaism. I identify with the Jewish people on a deep emotional and intellectual level. I would be able to transmit the essential values to my children easily, thereby making them strong and enriching their lives.

People tend to adopt the values, lifestyle, and beliefs of the majority culture in which they live. Christianity and Islam are the most popular of world religions and therefore the most accessible to newcomers in search of a faith. There is no doubt that one can readily find spiritual comfort in these religions and, in many instances, become a better person.

I would like my children to be Jewish. I would like them to identify with the very long and proud history of a people that refused to assimilate into the majority culture and that refused to spread their religion through fear, force, or bloodshed. I would like my children to have a very deep well from which to draw spiritual nourishment and practical guidance. Above all, I would like to ensure that *access to Judaism be safeguarded* for all future generations of humanity.

Belinda remarked that, though she could not relate to many of the ideas, she sensed that this essay was deeply important to me. I showed it to a Jewish friend. He liked it a lot, and he noted something interesting: there was no reference to *God*.

Challenging My Family

The next time my parents came to visit me in Toronto, I tried to take a daring step forward in breaking the ice. I invited my parents out for lunch at an elegant restaurant in Chinatown. I told Belinda I wanted her to meet my parents, but I would introduce her only as a friend. The day seemed to go well, although I was quite tense. At one point, after the meal, my father turned to me abruptly and remarked in Yiddish, "We hope you find somebody Jewish like her." I was elated! They liked her!

Eventually my parents were to find out that my interest in Belinda was more serious. When this happened, they urged me to end the relationship immediately unless there was a clear sign that she would convert. Moreover, as far as my parents were concerned, if Belinda really loved me, she would adopt Judaism for me, and if she didn't want to become Jewish, she probably didn't love me.

My father asked me in a letter whether I would consider marrying someone not Jewish. I dreaded the question. Skirting around it, I replied that for me, getting married was a holy act, not just a legal one, and that I could not see myself merely having a civil ceremony. Furthermore, I would not want to get married in a church.

This was an honest statement. I also knew that, should Belinda or her family want us, let's suppose, to get married in a Buddhist temple, then, unless they could convince me that Buddhism was the path to enlightenment, there would also have to be a ceremony at a synagogue. How this could be accomplished without Belinda converting to Judaism I didn't know, as rabbis did not generally officiate mixed marriages.[5] Therefore, I could not see myself "getting married"—in the technical sense of the expression—to someone not Jewish. This, of course, did not preclude *wanting* to get married to Belinda even if she did not convert, or perhaps living together (although Belinda was opposed to such a concept). As I struggled with my father's question, I became keenly aware of how deeply I felt about honouring my Jewish heritage now that it was being threatened.

5.   Increasingly, rabbis of the more liberal Jewish denominations, particularly in the United States, officiate mixed marriages, and I kept that in the back of my mind.

Despite the fact that the relationship had been stimulating my interest in Judaism, and Belinda and I had been inspiring each other toward spiritual growth, my parents continued to oppose my dating her.

They argued that the Chinese people and culture were unknown to them. My parents did not know what kind of sentiments either she or her family might harbour toward Jews. Were I ten years younger, my father counselled me, I would have the luxury of time to date Belinda and get to know her and her family better. However, time was at a premium and the current relationship might not work out in the end.

Furthermore, my parents wanted Jewish in-laws, like-minded people they could relate to and with whom they could celebrate Jewish events. Such ethnic affiliation was deemed important for their son, too.

Finally, should the marriage not work out (God forbid), then Belinda would presumably acquire custody of our children and raise them with her native culture and beliefs, rather than continue their Jewish education. Again, the assumption was that Belinda would become Jewish for the sake of love and marriage, but if these were to dissolve there would be little reason for her to continue living as a Jew.

This last factor may explain why my parents became anxious and impatient about Belinda's ambivalence with respect to conversion. The longer the relationship dragged on without Belinda's declaring her intention to convert, the greater was their suspicion that she did not truly love me and was probably just hanging on to me as a companion.

Their distrust stemmed undoubtedly from bewilderment. My parents couldn't fathom how it could take so long for *anyone* to make up her mind whether to become Jewish and get married. I couldn't blame them. There was something they couldn't understand, something fundamental and awesome that they would learn only over time and with growing frustration: *what becoming Jewish really entailed.*

I, too, was perplexed, but for another reason. I thought that if my parents so opposed my dating Belinda because she was not Jewish, then they must value Judaism greatly. If so, why did they complain that I was growing Jewishly? Why did it bother them when I eventually stopped driving or answering the phone on the holy Shabbos? Apparently Judaism, for my parents, was different from what it was quickly becoming for me. For them, Judaism was primarily the culture and the language rather than God-consciousness and strict adherence to our Torah. The latter contained potential for fanaticism. What they did not know, and what I was discovering, was that as far as traditional rabbis were concerned, conversion to Judaism required above all a total commitment to God's laws rather than immersion in a particular "Jewish" culture or language, much of which varies anyway from one Jewish community to the next.

I remember how my parents would inquire about our friends, teachers, and people in our lives as my siblings and I were growing up. It is normal for caring and responsible parents to take an interest in whom their children associate with, and my parents are the epitome of caring and responsible people. A frequent question would be, "Is he (or she) Jewish?" Although I was allowed to have non-Jewish friends, there seemed to be an implicit message that it was preferable to associate with Jews rather than non-Jews.

Naturally, I came to perceive Judaism as an insular system. We may interact with gentiles in business; we should certainly be respectful and polite to them; but ultimately we have to be wary of becoming too friendly with them, lest we end up adopting their customs, too much of their culture, and even (God forbid) marrying them.

Belinda and I had been learning from lectures that, far from being insular, the Jewish people have an important mission in the world: to raise humanity's level of morality and bring about lasting world peace. Perhaps the centuries-long persecution suffered at the hands of the non-Jewish world has caused Jews to forget the importance of this mission and focus instead on their own survival. As a child I learned about such ideas, but they did not mean much to me. Now they were an important revelation.

My relationship with my parents would continue to deteriorate in the months ahead. This would reach its nadir when I would drive to Montreal, in September 1996, to spend Rosh HaShanah with them. Upon extending the invitation, my father told me, matter-of-factly, that it would be the last time he would have any contact with me until one of two things happened: I terminated the relationship with Belinda or Belinda declared that she intended to convert to Judaism.

Confronting the Future

The first movie I took Belinda to was *Schindler's List*. It was very important for me that she become aware of the Holocaust, as she had not been exposed to the concept of anti-Semitism when she was growing up. Indeed, she had never even heard the term. The Nazis murdered my father's entire family, among six million Jews. In fact, between 1939 and 1945 two-thirds of the Jews of Eastern Europe (one-third of the world's Jewish population) were systematically annihilated for no other reason than that they were Jews. This had a tremendous impact on the psyche and worldview of every single surviving Jew as well as on their children and grandchildren. Many became more religious; others turned completely atheistic.

As a result — though not quite sure how — of dating a gentile, I became intensely interested in learning more about the horrors that my parents' generation had suffered. A few months later, Belinda and I drove to Washington with some friends to visit the recently-built Holocaust Museum.

I did not see or hear or learn anything drastically new, but I cried harder than I had ever cried before. For Belinda the exhibitions were eye-opening and shocking. The mountain of shoes and the pile of well-preserved eyeglasses that were once worn by a mere minuscule percentage of the victims; the children's drawings of butterflies and sunshine and unfulfilled dreams; the testimonies of survivors, interrupted constantly by sobbing — all this created a lasting impression in her consciousness.

From the very beginning of our relationship I looked for ways of sharing the beauty of my Jewish culture and heritage with Belinda, all the while discovering more and more of it myself. Early on Belinda told me that she liked the sound of my Yiddish name, Yankl. So I started using it, within the Jewish community, instead of my English name, Jack.

I was also very interested in Belinda's culture. We would go to Chinatown to eat, shop, or explore. I was fascinated with the Chinese language and constantly asked Belinda to teach me new words. It wasn't long before I could manage to string together a few simple sentences, and I enjoyed trying them out on Belinda's family, friends, and even Chinese waiters and salespeople that we encountered.

Alongside the exhilaration of being thrown into an alien culture, a melancholic undercurrent began to fester in me. Unlike Belinda, I didn't have family in Toronto, only friends. In my developing relationship with Belinda, it looked as if her parents, siblings, uncle, aunt, and a few cousins would become my surrogate relatives.

Mid-August Moon Festival, Chinese New Year, attending Buddhist temple — all were very interesting, but I was not sure whether I wanted to participate in them *on a regular*

Belinda and I explore Toronto's Chinatown

basis. Were any of the Buddhist practices idol worship?
Was I a heretic, betraying my Jewish heritage? Did it matter
whether our future children ate shrimp and pork, foods that
were obviously not kosher? Was it important that we abstain
from eating bread during the eight days of Passover, as I had
experienced growing up? Indeed, was my discomfort with
respect to all these issues the result of years of brainwashing
and guilt induced by my parents, school, and community?

Uneasy thoughts invaded my mind as I gazed across the buffet
table at Belinda and her uncle and aunt enjoying delicacies

unfamiliar to me. If I married Belinda, our children would live in two starkly different worlds — even more than I had done growing up with an Italian mother and a Polish father. At least both my parents were Jewish; at least the holidays, calendar, and lifecycle rites were basically the same. Yes, we *could* celebrate Rosh HaShanah, Passover, and Hanukkah along with the Mid-August Moon Festival, Chinese New Year, and the Dragon Boat Festival. We *could* speak Yiddish and Cantonese at home. We *could* enjoy foods from both traditions and vacation in Israel one year and Hong Kong the next. But it seemed that some of the most important things were mutually exclusive: would we be married in a Buddhist temple or in a synagogue? Would our final resting place be in a Chinese cemetery or a Jewish one? If *Yom Kippur* coincided with a Chinese festival or an important family celebration, would I be pressured to go for dim sum with Belinda's relatives, or would my conscience compel me to spend the day in synagogue absorbed in fasting and prayer?

Confronted with an ancient, rich, and fascinating Chinese tradition I knew nothing about, and which threatened to eclipse my own, I was challenged to identify what was ultimately unique and special about my Jewishness. I was forced to differentiate the essence of Judaism from its cultural echoes in which I had been immersed my entire life.

꼿

One evening I took Belinda to one of my favourite Italian restaurants. During the meal the conversation drifted to the approaching winter holiday season.

"Although I once sat on Santa's lap in our local mall, we never had a Christmas tree growing up," I mentioned casually.

"Really?" Belinda looked at me as if I were from Mars.

"Yeah, nor would I want a tree if we ever got married."

"Why not?"

I felt I was projecting intolerance, and I privately scolded myself. "We had Hanukkah, and there are other special and meaningful Jewish holidays for the whole family to enjoy," I replied. "We just don't do Christmas."

Belinda's eyes widened. Although she was not a Christian, and most of her family and relatives in Hong Kong were not Christians, they always celebrated Christmas. It had become an almost universal practice, bonding neighbours and communities, and it had nothing to do with Jesus.

"I thought *everyone* celebrated Christmas," she said.

"Actually, you'd be surprised how many people in North America don't. Then again, because we are so surrounded by the pretty lights and catchy tunes, it's tempting to get caught up in the holiday spirit, and many Jews do. You know, good will toward others...universal love...a happy time for family reunions...fun and presents for the kids. Who could argue against *that?*"

Belinda's complexion dimmed as her forehead tilted toward the table. She became very still. I realized that she must have fond childhood memories of Christmas, and it would be unfair if we were to light Hanukkah candles, sing Hanukkah songs, and eat the traditional potato pancakes — all of *my* fond childhood memories — and not have a Christmas tree. I decided then and there that there was nothing wrong with having a Christmas tree as long as we didn't ascribe religious significance to it and made it clear to our children that we didn't believe in Jesus.

"I guess if you really, really want a Christmas tree we should probably have one," I conceded.

Testing the Community

A prominent member of an Orthodox synagogue approached Belinda after Shabbos services and said, "I noticed you have been coming here regularly. Do you want to become Jewish?"

"I want to find the Truth," she replied.

When Belinda and I first met, we were both living in bachelor apartments in downtown Toronto. There was little by way of Jewish infrastructure in the area. Half of my friends were secular Jews, and the others were of diverse ethnicities. I was unaffiliated with any synagogue, and I had no *mezuzah* on my front doorpost. A month later Belinda moved into a small bungalow that she had purchased for her family. Her parents and younger siblings would be emigrating from Hong Kong prior to the 1997 Communist takeover, via a sponsorship agreement that Belinda undertook. Little did

Belinda know that, upon moving into her new home, she would be at the border of a major Jewish community and within a ten-minute walk from *The Village Shul*, a synagogue affiliated with *Aish HaTorah*, a highly successful Orthodox outreach[6] organization.

One sunny afternoon, just as Belinda and I stepped out of a non-kosher restaurant near the synagogue, I saw Rabbi Silver. He was a young, slim, clean-shaven, Orthodox rabbi whom I knew superficially through a monthly discussion group to which a friend had introduced me a year before I met Belinda.

He was standing a few feet away, in his characteristically self-assured posture, looking around as if trying to figure out in which direction he wanted to proceed. Instinctively I disengaged my hand from Belinda's and in one breath whispered to her that I knew this guy, he was a rabbi, she was not to extend her hand to him, and I would explain later.

After greeting Rabbi Silver and reminding him who I was, I felt compelled to introduce "my friend." We exchanged further pleasantries. Before parting he handed me his phone number and asked me to call him.

It took weeks until I mustered the courage.

---

6. Orthodox Jewish outreach organizations try to draw Jews closer to the teachings and practices of Judaism; they do not seek adherents from outside the Jewish fold.

I located a *kippa* at home and drove to our scheduled appointment on a rainy weekday evening. I had not been inside a rabbi's house in years. I was impressed by the elegance of his home and even more by the number of books on the shelves, including oversized, holy-looking ones. I wondered how such a young rabbi — perhaps only a few years older than I — had time to read so much, especially with a family to look after.

We both knew the purpose of the meeting. After chatting briefly about his book collection, our family backgrounds, and my knowledge of Yiddish and Italian, we got down to business.

"I was stunned to see you holding hands with an Oriental woman," Rabbi Silver began.

"She's from Hong Kong. I've known her for a few months. We became good friends."

"But she's not Jewish, right?"

"Correct, she's currently not Jewish. But she doesn't have any other religion. Anyway, we have a lot in common. I've dated many Jewish women in my life and found most of them materialistic. Belinda is honest, down-to-earth—"

"I'm sure she's an exceptional lady. Listen, although it may be very difficult to believe, there *is* somebody Jewish out there for you; you need only have patience and you will find your *bashert* (match)."

"Belinda knows almost nothing about Judaism; however, she doesn't harbour the slightest anti-Semitic sentiments." I spoke defensively. "Moreover, she is interested in learning more about our heritage."

"It may be good that she's interested in learning about Judaism, but learning about Judaism and becoming a Jew are two very different things. She doesn't have to become Jewish. Gentiles are assured a place in heaven as long as they are decent people."

"I know that—I learned it in high school. But Belinda needs the opportunity to experience Judaism. She *deserves* it." I was now on the offensive. "The Reform rabbis welcomed us to their events. Would you consider having us over for a Shabbos meal sometime?" I asked with trepidation.

"I'm afraid I'd be indisposed to doing so," came the immediate response. "However, *you* are welcome to join us the week after next."

When he saw me get up to leave, he retracted. "Let me talk to my wife, and if she agrees, we could have you both over—*but on one condition:* that you promise to break off the relationship immediately afterward."

I thought it over for a moment, and a feeling of indignation swept over me. "I'm not prepared to make such a promise. I want *three* Orthodox Shabbos experiences with Belinda before I would consider ending the relationship."

Rabbi Silver refused to negotiate. I thanked him for his time, and went home.

The meeting left a bitter taste and confirmed something about Orthodox rabbis that I had long suspected: they are not keen on giving gentiles entry to Judaism.

I wanted Belinda to feel a comfort with Judaism that books and lectures alone cannot provide. People and community, by contrast, have the power to make one feel like an alien trespassing on holy ground or like a welcome visitor wanting innocently to find out whether the terrain one is exploring is suitable for building one's new home. Since the beginning of our relationship, our idea had been to take the best of both our worlds for ourselves and our future family. Because Belinda's appearance put her at a serious disadvantage in a Jewish environment, I felt all the more the need to defend her right of access to my heritage.

I began to think of myself as an advocate for gentiles' entering to Judaism. It irked me that while the evangelical Protestant movement was aggressively and successfully reaching out to thousands, if not millions, of Chinese people who lacked any strong religious ties — winning over Belinda's brother and younger sister in the process — there was not the least amount of interest on the part of rabbis to attract anyone outside the tiny Jewish fold. In the global marketplace of religions, Orthodox Judaism seemed to bury its self-assured head in the sand.

A friend, whose intellectual honesty and abilities I respected, recounted how, as a teenager, he had rejected his native Sikh religion and embarked on an elaborate search for meaning. He examined religion after religion before concluding that Sikhism actually made the most sense. I asked him what he thought about Judaism. "That's one religion I didn't investigate," he replied, much to my dismay. Because he had examined Christianity, he explained, he figured that there was no need to study Judaism separately, for the Old Testament was incorporated within the newer Christian faith.

This angered me. Things are not always what they are made to seem. I thought of my father and his campaign for Yiddish. Though I was fortunate to have been exposed to the inner beauties of Yiddish, most young people saw our linguistic and cultural heritage through a very distorted lens. Why was it that the few Yiddish words or expressions that many in my age bracket knew, were negative: *khazeray* (junk food); *kvetch* (nag); *meshuge* (crazy); *fardreyt* (confused); *shmatte* (rag); *ganef* (thief); and *tsores* (troubles)? How could a generation of North American Jews grow up perceiving a very rich and expressive language to be inadequate, even laughable?

Belinda's interest in Judaism was piqued through a series of weekly lectures that began in March 1995 under the auspices of *Ohr Somayach*, a sister organization to Aish HaTorah. Some time before, I had come across a notice in the *Canadian Jewish News* about the opening of a new Ohr Somayach learning centre downtown. The catchy title of the talk at the inaugural event was "Torah and the Art of Motorcycle Maintenance."

I invited Belinda to join me, anticipating some Zen connection.

Neither Belinda nor I recall what the lecture was about, except that it had nothing to do with Buddhism. Rabbi Burowitz captivated the audience with his informative and highly entertaining speech. Boosted by the feedback, he followed up with a series of free weekly lectures on such topics as free will, prayer, sexuality, Shabbos, and Jewish observance.

Belinda and I took the opportunity of the small class size — only about a dozen people attended — to ask many questions. Belinda was persistent in seeking logically satisfying answers. Her pointed questions were not tainted by any stereotypes of Orthodox Judaism, and her assessment of the rabbi's responses were not filtered through any particular disdain or affinity for the Jewish people. Her questions were logical and objective and came from a fresh perspective. I benefited considerably from her exchanges with Rabbi Burowitz.

One Wednesday evening, after parking near the centre, I was about to get out of the car when Belinda asked what the hurry was. Glancing at my watch, I acknowledged that we were a few minutes early for the lecture. Belinda asked if we could sit and listen to soft music on the radio. On another Wednesday evening she insisted that we walk around the block before entering the building. Eventually it dawned on me that she preferred to wait until the last minute before going to the class. She admitted that she was self-conscious being the only visible non-Jew.

Once, as we hastily walked to our seats just as the lecture was starting, someone called out, "Your wife?" indicating my Chinese girlfriend. I shook my head and took my seat, feeling the uncomfortable gaze of half the people present. "My sister" is what I *wished* I had responded, as I tried to focus on the lecture!

One week Belinda had to miss a class, so I went by myself. Rabbi Flanz, who worked at the centre, approached me and inquired where I lived. He said he would like to invite me for a Shabbos meal sometime, leaving the date unspecified. I thanked him and asked if he knew of my Chinese girlfriend. He replied that he had noticed her a couple of times in the building. I asked if she would be welcome as well. "It may be possible." I sensed that he preferred that I come alone.

Spurred by the desire to grow Jewishly, and wishing to be closer to my girlfriend, I began to look for a bachelor apartment in the heart of the religious Jewish community. Soon I found one in a building known as "the vertical *shtetl*" (*shtetl* means a small Eastern European town).

Soon after that, Belinda and I had our first authentic Shabbos experience together. It was at the home of Rabbi Flanz. By now I lived within a five-minute walk of his home. The Flanzes were very hospitable. To our pleasant surprise, the rabbi's wife served us Chinese food and handed us chopsticks. We talked non-stop about Shabbos, Judaism, and everything under the sun. When it was finally time to leave, the rabbi accompanied us for half a block, a gesture that struck me as unusually amiable. At one point, when Belinda was out of earshot, he said to me, out of the blue, "You know, I used to believe Jewish continuity was the reason not to intermarry." With that perplexing statement, he turned around, thanked us again for coming, and left.

It was a long time later that I learned Orthodox Judaism is ultimately not concerned about Jewish continuity. It assumes God will ensure the survival of the Jewish people (however small in number) *no matter what*. Rather, the reason not to intermarry was as plain and simple as it was problematical: because God said so.

❧

In the fall of 1995, Belinda and I started meeting at the Village Shul on many Shabbos mornings, while continuing to explore other religions as well.

Belinda was self-conscious every time she stepped into this tiny storefront synagogue. I, too, was uncomfortable — being seen with her. Many of the congregants wore black hats; the praying was intensive; and the atmosphere felt foreign. Moreover, Belinda knew by then that interdating was frowned upon, and I half-expected some rabbi or prominent member of the synagogue to ask her, or both of us, to leave. Belinda could not hide the fact that she was not Jewish; were she an Orthodox convert, her dress would have been more modest and her mannerisms more assured.

In fact, we didn't go there for prayer. We went for the classes that were being offered concurrently with the services. Each

Shabbos one of the rabbis would lead a discussion on different ideas in Judaism, such as the beauty and significance of Shabbos, appreciation of God, or the purpose of prayer. The classes were free and quite enlightening. Afterward people would stay for *Kiddush*, a Shabbos prayer chanted over wine, followed by a period of socializing over refreshments. Initially, we left as soon as the class was over and did not stay for Kiddush. Over time, as we got to know some of the people and became more familiar with the Jewish concepts that were being disseminated, we felt more welcome and stayed longer.

Sometimes people approached me privately with an invitation to come to their homes for lunch. Before accepting I would nervously and somewhat challengingly ask if "my friend" was welcome as well. The answer would invariably be yes.

Over time, we got to know people better and felt more comfortable in this synagogue. The atmosphere took on a warm and friendly glow. However, our objective, whether in the synagogue or in people's homes, was to learn more about Judaism rather than to make friends or fit in.

At a certain level, I felt that if I could disprove the Orthodox rabbis' grand claim of knowing how God wants Jews to live — what they may eat, whom they should marry, when and how they must pray — I would be free to live as I wished. I might still not have found the formula for mending the world, but at least I could marry my sweetheart and settle down.

The observant Jewish lifestyle was a heavy chain that threatened to hook itself onto my navel, becoming a new umbilical cord, this time for life. Just learning the laws would require considerable time and effort. And once learned, putting them into practice and integrating them into my comfortable and familiar lifestyle seemed daunting.

That I was dating a non-Jewish woman while attending an Orthodox synagogue was constantly on my mind. I wondered how judgmental the members of the synagogue and broader religious Jewish community were, and I frequently engaged people in dialogue about my situation. When I specifically asked if I should be dating Belinda, typical responses were "It's not ideal," "I wouldn't do it," and "You have to make your own decision." However, the vast majority of respondents indicated that if Belinda continued to show an interest in Judaism and eventually converted in a proper manner, there should be nothing wrong with my marrying her.

Some people in the community advised me to end the relationship. I was told that even if Belinda converted, our Chinese-looking children would be mocked in the school playground. I was reminded that, unlike other children who may have eminent Jewish lineages to brag about through both parents, ours would certainly not. Furthermore, once our children had learned of all the horrible things that gentiles had done to the Jews throughout the ages, they would be embarrassed.

One religious person even suggested that a convert should only marry another convert. Although I generally welcome the opinions of others, I reacted viscerally. First and foremost, I told him, Jews are one people. We express it all the time in our prayers. What better way of demonstrating that we truly subscribe to this principle than by accepting and welcoming a convert from an entirely different race and culture? Either we are one people with one mission, one history and one destiny, or we are not. If we are not, then our "Judaism" is nothing more than an ethnic identity. We know of Indian Jews, Ethiopian Jews, Spanish Jews, and Russian Jews. There were once hundreds of Chinese Jews as well, with their rabbis and thriving communities.[7] To discriminate based on skin colour or other racial features is clearly racist and, in fact, anti-Jewish.

Throughout our tumultuous history, I continued, we lived among different peoples, adopting their languages, their dress, their architecture, their customs. In the course of the past 3,300 years, we dressed in ways that we no longer do, spoke languages that we no longer speak, enjoyed foods that we no longer eat. Indeed, our history, from a cultural point of view, is fragmented. Yet we survived as a people because the Torah and our commitment to it have remained intact.

Once started on this line of thinking, I continued to ponder the potential benefits should Belinda and I marry. By being exposed to different cultures, my children might be inclined to look for that which is deeper and more important. They would be less likely to mistake culture for religion; to equate the significance of *latkes* with *menorah*. The former is temporal and confined to particular geography, the latter is everlasting and universally meaningful among Jews.

7.   The communities, centred in Kaifeng, China, had all but disappeared by the mid-1800s.

Yes, if Belinda and I got married, many Jews might look upon us curiously, even mock us. After all, a Chinese Jew is a rare phenomenon. However, those who understand the true essence of Judaism (and all good and sensitive people) would respect us. They might even be flattered that a Chinese woman chose to take on such a tremendous responsibility, despite her deep attachment to her family and her secular upbringing.

"My great grandfather was a famous Torah scholar. What about yours?" Kids (and, unfortunately, adults too) have a tendency to brag about their lineage and are often envious of each other. Such behaviour and attitude are poisonous and contrary to the values of Judaism. If it should happen that our children were teased at *yeshiva* (religious school) because of their Chinese appearance or their family history, it would invite the opportunity to learn, in a real and tangible way, some of the most important lessons that, indeed, any child is expected to learn in yeshiva: to love one's fellow Jew; not to hurt others in word or deed; and that Judaism is *above* one's outward appearance or heritage. Abraham's father was an idol worshipper. Also, the Torah points out that the Messiah will come from the line of King David, who was a descendent of the convert, Ruth.

Though the Chinese constitute roughly one-fifth of humanity, the percentage that knows anything about Judaism is surprisingly low. Belinda's family and relatives, typically, were quite ignorant about Judaism; however, they had nothing against Jews or their religion. Of all the peoples of the world, the Chinese are one of the few peoples that historically have been friendly toward the Jews and exhibited virtually no anti-Semitism. Traditional Chinese culture tends to be tolerant of different religions.

Not only could we be of benefit to others by virtue of our racially mixed family, but we would also have much to gain ourselves. At times, in Orthodox circles, Judaism is lived out mechanically. By being in contact with Belinda's family and relatives, who have a different worldview, Belinda and I would continually have the opportunity to critically examine our way of life and reinvigorate our Judaism. We would be free to deepen our commitment to our faith without fear of becoming insular. By interacting with close non-Jewish family, Belinda and I and our children would be forced to enhance our sensitivity toward the non-Jewish world. We would then avoid the mistake of thinking that Jews were superior to non-Jews.

In a lighter vein, I sometimes mused about other benefits of marrying Belinda: Chinese food every day...a lot of time saved looking for my wife in large Jewish crowds...

Finally, it may be true that it is generally easier to raise children when both parents are from the same cultural background. On the other hand, life is not about ease and comfort, but about challenge and growth. I concluded that as long as Belinda and I were aware of the many challenges that lay ahead as a result of our unique situation and were willing to commit our best efforts, our life together could be a rewarding adventure.

3

Changing Lenses

*I*n the neighbourhood where I grew up, the vast majority of Jews were affiliated with the Orthodox denomination of Judaism. This was partly by default, as the Conservative and Reform movements were not well established in Montreal. Although we attended Orthodox synagogues, most of us were fairly assimilated and did not follow many of the laws prescribed in the Torah. In contrast were the Hassidic Jews, who lived in other neighbourhoods. They were easily recognized by their distinctive dress, and they typified for me what "religious Jews" were.

Looking at these Hassidic Jews, as I did, from the "outside in," I saw them walking about in the dead heat of summer in their long black frocks and round fur hats, presenting a mildly depressing image. They were very insular, cut off from the rest of the world, having little awareness and interest in anything outside their "cult." They did not watch television or listen to the radio. Although they had their own newspapers (mostly in Yiddish), they certainly never attended a movie or sports event. In late afternoons one sometimes saw tired, pale-faced children taking the bus home from yeshiva. These youngsters, albeit unusually well mannered, were deprived of play, exercise, and fresh air, having been forced to study all day in a stuffy environment and strain their eyes on the tiniest of Hebrew print. Praying and learning the Torah were the most cherished things in life for Hassidic Jews, more so than physical well-being.

Hassidic Jews appeared to me passive and naive. In the face of difficulty or disaster, they pray to God for help instead of taking remedial action. They follow a highly structured, rigid, and complex code of conduct. Whenever they have a question about even the most trivial detail of their lives, they run to their *rebbe* (teacher) for guidance. In essence, they abdicate their decision-making to a higher authority and stop thinking for themselves. The religious lifestyle, I often mused, was best suited for the psychologically weak, as it helped to keep them out of trouble.

Of course, what I have just described is a rather distorted image of religious Jews. In retrospect, I realize that I knew very little about their intricate and fascinating world and liberally applied my imagination to fill the gaps.

In contrast to the religious Jew — whom I regarded with a curious combination of disdain, ridicule, respect, and even admiration—I considered myself a "normal" or "middle-of-the-road" Jew. We would fast on Yom Kippur and even walk to synagogue. If it was raining hard, we did not rule out driving, even though this is prohibited. On Friday nights our family would usually gather around the table for a festive meal—which began typically with chicken soup or gefilte fish—and sometimes my father would recite the Kiddush prayer. We never ate pork or lobster or mixed meat and milk products together. However, except during Passover, other foods that we consumed did not have to be strictly kosher (we would eat at McDonald's, but wouldn't order cheeseburgers; or, if we did, we would remove the cheese before eating them).

Many of the laws of Judaism that we observed were kept because of habit or tradition. My mother, for instance, exempted us from house chores on Saturdays. She also did not allow us to trim our nails on that day, a restriction which, after several unsuccessful attempts at obtaining a logical explanation, I wrote off as a cultural idiosyncrasy that she inherited from her parents. Other things we did, such as fasting on Yom Kippur or conducting the Passover *Seder*, were additionally aimed at spiritual elevation.

Although I knew that some people believed we had to follow the laws because *God Himself* demanded it, I did not subscribe to this "archaic" view. My rational mind could not fathom why a Supreme Benevolent Being would command us to do things that so inconvenienced us. Moreover, many prohibitions that religious Jews follow, such as not switching lights on or off on Shabbos, I considered ludicrous. They were fabrications, manifestations of a proclivity to asceticism, and did not come from the Torah (electricity, after all, did not exist 3,300 years ago). Thus, while in many instances, for the sake of convenience, we bent the rules and made compromises on what we *knew* was the law because we did not believe it was the Divine Will, in some cases we were just simply ignorant of the law.[8]

For me, becoming observant was a radical option, although one I felt free to pursue, should I ever want to do so. In the meantime, while I lived at home, I was more or less content with my life and reasoned that I was not obligated to learn about and observe the myriad rules that religious Jews observed — after all, I was not a "religious" Jew.

Nevertheless, a few encounters with observant Jews scattered over the years left an imprint, a deep-felt attraction to their curious little world. When I was a teenager, my sister, who is ten years older than I am, became observant and immigrated to Israel. In the summer of 1989, during a backpacking tour of Europe and Israel, I took the opportunity to visit her. I had just stepped out of the washroom and was set to go about my activities, when my brother-in-law noticed me and inquired whether I had recited the blessing. *"Ayzeh berakhah?"* (What blessing?) I asked, perplexed. "The thanksgiving blessing that we are obligated to make upon exiting the washroom every time we relieve ourselves," he returned in Hebrew. I was stunned. My brother-in-law guided me through the ancient words. Basically, we thank the Creator for having fashioned us

8. During Shabbos, creating a spark, which in essence is what happens when an electric circuit is completed, is clearly prohibited by the Torah.

wisely, and for creating within us many openings and cavities, any one of which, if it were ruptured or blocked, would not enable us to survive. I was captivated by the concept! In our busy lives, we take so much for granted, and here Judaism teaches us to pause and to appreciate the delicate complexity and wondrousness of even as mundane a thing as our basic bodily functions.

"Do Not Judge Judaism by the Jews"

One day, I found myself on the wide cobblestone streets of a very religious enclave of Jerusalem. People were dressed in their finest clothes: men and boys in black hats and white shirts, women and girls in colourful, ankle-length dresses. Not a single car or bus was in motion. All the shops were closed. All business activity for the week had come to a standstill. People strode along the middle of the street as if they owned it and seemed without a care in the world. The air had become noticeably cooler and more pleasant. The atmosphere was charged with anticipation. I needed to get to my sister's place before the onset of Shabbos.

I glanced at my watch. In the past half hour a multitude of people, mostly men, had spilled onto the street and were hurrying in all directions, sometimes greeting one another in Yiddish or Hebrew as they passed: "Good Shabbos." Feeling out of place in a strange community, and not looking particularly Jewish (I was not wearing a head covering), I had held off disturbing people for directions, convincing myself that I could manage on my own. But now the sun was about to set. Remembering my promise to my sister that I would arrive early, I began to sweat and move about frantically. I signalled to a group of gentlemen. They slowed down a little and one or two muttered something about being in a hurry to attend the synagogue services. I don't know if they even heard my question. I felt angry and disappointed as I watched them walk away: angry at the fact that praying to God was more important to them than helping a fellow Jew; disappointed because this was not the superior religious approach to life my sister and brother-in-law described.

About a year before I met Belinda, Rabbi Silver, after listening to me complain numerous times about Orthodox Jews, said to me, "Do not judge Judaism by the Jews." I often meditated on that statement. Jewish people are human and therefore not perfect. At the same time, there are countless observant Jews who are outstanding role models and exemplify character refinement at its best. To the extent that religious people (in *any* faith) do not behave properly, one can question how "religious" they truly are. They may belong to a religious organization, don the religious garb, even practise the rituals and espouse all the beliefs—but if they do not care about their fellow people, are not honest in their business dealings, or are otherwise self-centred, one must ask whether this is what the religious teachings expect of them.

Tenuous Enlightenment

After light stretching, Belinda and I assumed the half-lotus position on the grass, eyes closed, our faces warmed by the mid-day sun. This contorted posture, I explained, "grounded" us, connecting us to the planet and its inhabitants. We had located a quiet part of the park. I led us into meditation, wherein we attempted to relax every part of our bodies using a visualization technique. I spoke softly, trying to mimic the soothing tone and inflections of my Yoga teacher.

Belinda was open to the experience. She had taken a few sessions of Yoga, as well as Tai Chi, which had been offered at her workplace. She said it helped improve her well-being.

"Relaxation is the key to living a healthy and happy life," I remarked when we re-opened our eyes. "Even at work I have more energy and can accomplish more when I relax."

"Yeah, I feel the same way."

"All of us live with some tension and anxiety," I continued pedantically. "We have an underlying sense of fear."

"Fear of what?"

"Losing what we have. We cling on to our job, our possessions, our prestige, because they give us a feeling of security. Eastern philosophies, however, teach that we must become aware of our attachments and learn to let go of them, so that temptations can no longer have power over us. We then become free to live the kind of life we really want."

"It's funny that you should teach *me* Eastern philosophy. In Chinese, we say *'mo yoh mo kau'* — when one has no desire, one has no need," Belinda offered.

71

Doing yoga in a park

"And therefore no stress," I added. "Of course, you can't just force yourself to let go, you need specific techniques and disciplines—like breathing, for example." I leaned over toward Belinda and showed her how to breath more slowly and deeply, and more consciously. "Learning to control our breathing helps untie old tensions that have been locked into the muscles. It also trains us to live in the moment, which is a vital ingredient in happiness. Most of us live in the past or in the future. We miss out on life, which is a continuous flow of *nows*."

I was on a roll, and Belinda felt it. "These are the kinds of things they teach you at the ashram?" she asked.

"Yes, but they're also from my own reflections over the years. Anyway, it's wonderful to have a community of people that shares the same attitudes and outlook. On Friday evenings, after stretching and meditation, we enjoy a healthy, delicious vegetarian supper. Then we sit on the floor in a circle and share things we are grateful for in the previous week, anything unusual that happened to us, or any new insights into life. We take turns reading inspiring stories. We dance wildly to mantra-like music. It nourishes the soul." I felt I had a lot of wisdom to impart and hoped that Belinda would be receptive. It would be an important test of our compatibility. It had been one or two months since we had met.

"Bel, everything you need to know is within you. Our bodies have their own wisdom whose source is the cosmic energy that surrounds us. This energy unites us with others and, indeed, with all things. So all we really need to do is relax and trust in the wisdom of the Universe, that the Universe will take care of itself. If we tune into this cosmic flow then our feelings and reactions, instead of being automatic and predictable, will become more spontaneous. We will naturally do what is good and proper."

"You sound idealistic. It's almost too good to be true."

At this point, I chided myself for trying to convey too many concepts all at once. I began rubbing together the palms of my hands. I held them out in front of my chest, facing each other — first one inch apart, then two inches, then three inches, and eventually six inches apart. For the next two minutes, I stared at my hands and concentrated intensely.

"Now, take your right hand and pass it slowly through the space between my palms," I instructed my girlfriend.

"That's it...Did you notice anything?" I hoped that I wasn't about to make a fool of myself.

"*Amazing*...I think I felt something."

"What did you feel? What was it?"

"It felt like...like heat, but it *wasn't* heat. There was some tingling sensation. I can't describe it!"

"What you felt was energy," I let out delightedly. "I have learned to channel energy at will. It's a universal healing energy. It's what I've been talking about."

"Interesting. I guess you like going to the Centre."

"Actually, there are a few things that I don't like about the place. For one thing, I don't agree with bowing to the feet of the guru—or his picture. I am the only one who remains perfectly still in the hall while everyone else lowers their head to the floor."

"Why don't you bow?"

"I think it's dangerous to treat another person like a god. No one is perfect, not even Moses was. It's a fundamental idea in Judaism. In fact, I've written a letter to the guru. I said that it would be better to bow to his books and tapes than to him.

He never replied. I have no problem venerating wisdom, but I refuse to worship another human being."

Belinda looked at me intently.

"Here's another thing I have a big problem with. It seems that many people in the Centre subscribe to the notion of *ahimsa* — non-violence in any circumstance. It may have worked for Ghandi, but I believe a major lesson of the Holocaust is that there are times when we must fight and defend ourselves from evil with militant force. I don't buy into the proposition that every person is inherently good, that you can change *anyone's* evil behaviour with love. So, Bel, I am divided: I really like a lot of the teachings and practices of the Yoga community, but I can't get myself fully into it, even though I have been going to the Centre for several years."

"I think your Jewish upbringing had an effect on you."

"Probably more than I realize. But I really wish Judaism could incorporate some of the Eastern teachings. Judaism appears so ethnocentric. And lifeless — like cold, stale bread. Speaking of food: When we go to Jewish lectures, they always seem to have pop, chips, or salted pretzels as refreshments. I hate that. I once asked a rabbi about it, why they can't put out juice and celery sticks instead."

"What did he say?"

"He said it was for practical reasons: healthy foods cost more, take longer to prepare, and need a fridge for storage. He agreed with me that the body is a temple, and that ideally we should not be consuming junk food. He was obviously being apologetic, but it wasn't good enough. I should have asked him, 'what if it were more economical and convenient to eat pork chops?' but I didn't want to offend him."

"I guess for rabbis, eating kosher is more important than keeping your body healthy," Belinda said matter-of-factly.

"It seems that way. Hey, maybe you and I should start a new religion, a combination of Buddhism and Judaism. Taking the best of both worlds."

"I'm all for it!" Belinda returned. "We'll call it...*Buddaism.*"

We both laughed.

Exploring Different Religions

Soon after Belinda and I met we started to explore various religions together. We attended church services, a Protestant evangelical "mission," a Chinese Taoist–Christian conversion ceremony (where, for a fee of $10, we became "Christian Taoists" within a few hours and received a "passport to heaven"), a Sikh Gurdwara, Buddhist temples, a Mosque, as well as Jewish Reform, Conservative, and Orthodox synagogues and events. We talked to people at every opportunity and read a lot. At one point I had a tall stack of books on my desk, each one on a different religion.

One time we attended Friday night services at a Jews for Jesus temple. Afterward, everyone gathered in the social hall where we sang, and I accompanied popular Hebrew songs on the piano. On another occasion, Belinda and I met with the director for several hours and debated whether one can be a fully practicing Jew and at the same time accept Jesus as one's personal saviour.

Although far from being an orderly process, our examination and rational reflections over the next two years gradually led us to believe that Torah Judaism was *closer to the Truth than any other religion*. Here are a few basic ideas that we discovered.

A story is told of a Hassidic boy who comes home from school one day proudly displaying to his mother a handful of candies that he received from his rebbe. The mother, stupefied but knowing that the teacher sometimes gave out a candy or two as a reward for correctly answering a difficult question, turned to her son and said, "You must have known the answer to a question that no one else in your class knew."

"No," replied the boy spiritedly, "I was the only one in my class who asked the teacher a question that *he* couldn't answer!"

Persistent questioning, discussing, and debating for the purpose of gaining clarity is not only encouraged in Judaism but is at the core of its pedagogical system. In yeshiva, students are routinely paired with a partner to study the sacred texts. They spend countless hours analyzing the most minute details of the subject matter, stretching their analytical abilities, and drawing on various Torah commentators from throughout the ages to formulate their contentions. If one were to step into their crowded study hall, one would not find a sign, as in a library, stating, "Quiet, please." Rather, one might be met by an impressive display of books, in Hebrew and Aramaic, sprawled open over long wooden tables, and a cacophony of animated discussions as students excitedly debate and argue their points.

By contrast, Belinda and I have been in religious settings where asking many questions was discouraged. For instance, I was taught, while learning Yoga, that one must follow one's heart and subjugate one's mind to it. At a time when I was hungry for answers and challenged certain practices and ideas with penetrating questions, the ashram leadership advised me to stop intellectualizing so much because the intellect tends to be an obstacle to attaining inner peace, harmony, and "true wisdom." In another situation, while attending a particular church (which, we later learned, was not mainstream in its views), Belinda, as usual, asked a lot of questions. Eventually she was rebuked: "You ask too many questions," "The demon is with you," and "God gets irritated by people like you."

❧

Besides the tremendous emphasis placed on learning and asking questions, Jews widely study the Bible in the original language. When Belinda and I attended Bible classes at our synagogue, the text we used was in Hebrew, with English translation on the opposite side of the pages. The translation was by a universally esteemed rabbi with an excellent command of both languages. Even so, the teacher would constantly shift back and forth between the Hebrew and the English, commenting on the subtle differences in nuance, pointing out additional connotations of words, and, in effect, showing us that in order to arrive at the deeper meaning of the text, it was *imperative* to understand the Hebrew. Having grown up speaking five languages, including Hebrew, I could appreciate how much is lost in even the best translations.

By contrast, whenever I came across a copy of the Christian Bible (New Testament and Old Testament), whether in a church, bookstore, or hotel room, the text would be exclusively in English. How, I wondered, could Truth-seeking Christians who did not know Hebrew, hope to understand the hidden lessons of Adam and Eve, the Flood, or the Ten Commandments?

But there was a bigger problem. I first became vaguely aware of it a few weeks after I met Belinda. She was sitting in her room reading the Christian Bible, possibly for the first time in her life. Noticing that she was almost at the end, I asked her, somewhat hesitantly, what she thought of the Bible. She responded that the "New Testament" made a lot more sense to her than the "Old Testament."[9] After my initial disappointment — I feared she was being drawn to Jesus — I said to myself, "Wait a minute. The Old and New Testaments are not supposed to be in competition with each other! If

9.   The terms "Hebrew Bible" and "Old Testament" are used in this section interchangeably for the sake of simplicity. In practice, Judaism does not refer to its Bible as the "Old Testament" because, from its viewpoint, it has not been replaced by any "new" Testament.

the Old Testament doesn't make sense, then how can the New Testament, *which is built on the presumed truth of the Old Testament,* make any more sense?"

Belinda was right. Numerous things, upon close examination, did not make sense in the Old Testament. From literary and editorial standpoints, the book is grossly deficient. It is laden with inexplicable digressions, redundancies, repetitiveness, logical omissions, and so on — hardly fitting of a work authored by God!

Judaism posits that the Oral Tradition is necessary to properly understand the Old Testament. Rather than present a finite reference manual that could gather dust on people's shelves, God presumably knew that the ultimate value of the Bible lay in its being passed down orally from generation to generation. The written Torah was merely the "condensed notes." Moral guidance would be inspired and reinforced by a living, breathing tradition, infused with endless layers of meaning, guided by context, and subject to innumerable caveats.

When the Oral Tradition is brought into play, things become remarkably clear. "An eye for an eye, a tooth for a tooth," for instance, does not mean what Christians generally think it means.[10] That Christianity does not delve into the Oral Tradition means, from the perspective of Judaism, that there is no way it can properly understand the Old Testament. Indeed, without the help of the Oral Tradition it is possible for people

10. It is clear from the Oral Tradition that the statement refers specifically to matters of monetary compensation. It is not intended to be taken literally as a means of bodily vengeance. (See the Babylonian Talmud, Bava Kamma, ch 8)

with enough creativity to interpret certain obscure passages in the Bible in almost any way they want.

The New Testament is the focus of Christian theology, with the Old Testament supposedly lending support to it. However, the Old Testament, *as understood by rabbis*, not only does not lend support to the New Testament — it contradicts it in fundamental ways. For Jews, the Hebrew Bible is the indisputable and irrefutable word of God, while the New Testament is a heretical invention by a sect of renegade Jews 2,000 years ago. However, for Christians, both are the word of God. Which approach is correct?

Let us assume, for example, that rabbis understand the Old Testament more correctly than do Christian theologians. This would cast doubt on the veracity of Christianity, whose main focus — the New Testament — hinges on Christian interpretation of the Old Testament. Conversely, if we assume that the Christian theologian's understanding of the Old Testament is more accurate, then the claims of Christianity vis-à-vis those of Judaism are strengthened.

Throughout the past 3,300 years, not only did rabbis know Hebrew (and pray in Hebrew), but they followed the exceedingly detailed and exacting laws pertaining to how a Torah scroll is to be copied; what renders a Torah scroll invalid (if even one letter of one word in the entire Torah scroll is missing or *shaped* wrong, that particular scroll is invalid and should not be used for public reading until corrected); the uncompromising manner in which the Torah portion was to be recited in synagogue (not a single word may be mispronounced or omitted); and the extraordinary care that must be taken in the physical handling of a Torah scroll. Such obsessive measures, aimed at safeguarding the Bible from being altered or tampered with in the slightest manner, are possibly unparalleled in other religions. This, combined with an equally rigorous system for accurately transmitting the Oral Tradition, helped persuade Belinda and me that what Judaism represented was more authentic than Christianity or any other religion that staked its truth on the Old Testament.

Judaism is the oldest living monotheistic religion. It claims that the Bible was presented simultaneously to well over a million people who stood at Mount Sinai, each of whom personally "witnessed the voice of God." It supposedly happened in this manner so that there could be no question as to the divine authenticity of the event.[11] Judaism, in fact, is the only religion that claims that an entire nation heard God speak. Most religions are started by individuals who claim that God spoke to them *personally* in a dream or vision. The other monotheistic religions — Christianity and Islam and their offshoots — recognize that the Jewish people possessed God's book and that they still possess it, intact and unchanged. They do not dispute the event at Mount Sinai. The only difference is that they claim that the Torah has been replaced and superseded by a newer covenant. Interestingly, as if anticipating the possibility of being tempted away from the

11. Every religious family has faithfully reported the event at Mount Sinai to their children since its occurrence 3,300 years ago. Nowhere is there any record of a mass conspiracy by an entire generation to deceive their children.

heavy demands of the Torah, the Torah itself explicitly tells us that its laws and ordinances are *eternally binding.*[12]

ꙅ

What about religions that did *not* base themselves on the Hebrew Bible? What about Hinduism or Buddhism, for example? And why should there be only one true religion, anyway? Maybe there could be more than one Truth.

Religious belief systems, as I understood, are based on fundamental assumptions about the nature of God, the nature of humankind, and events in the universe. The prescriptive dimension of every world religion — how people ought to behave and interact in this world — follows from its assumptions about reality. When religions differ and even contradict one another on such basic assumptions, then the religious paths, insofar as they hinge on these assumptions, cannot be equally valid.

In the religions that are not based on the Hebrew Bible, Belinda and I discovered a wealth of wisdom and beauty and practical insights for living. Nevertheless, we found their core theological assumptions problematic. To us, it made more sense that there is one God rather than multiple deities.[13] *God* meant the Creator of the universe — infinitely powerful, omniscient, and infinitely benevolent. Monotheism meant one

12. See, for example, Deuteronomy 4:1–2; and 13:1–6.
13. In Hinduism, Taoism, and Buddhism one finds references to their different deities being expressions of one God, or "God-head." This suggests some inclination toward monotheism even in these officially non-monotheistic religions.

ultimate source of authority, one standard of morality, one right and wrong. A universe of multiple deities, by contrast, presents multiple sources of authority, potentially multiple standards of morality, and multiple definitions of right and wrong. In paganism, various gods are often at war with each other and have strengths and weaknesses, particular needs and desires. Whereas, according to the Bible, God created humans in God's image, in the polytheistic religions the gods seemed to have been fashioned in the image of humankind!

In the ancient world, when one nation conquered another, the vanquished nation would adopt the deities of the conqueror. Along with the new deities came the adoption of a new lifestyle, new values, and perhaps new criteria of right and wrong. Thus in ancient Greece, during a period of time, it was considered proper to leave deformed babies on hilltops to die.[14] In Hindu India, for hundreds of years, a widow would join her husband on the funeral pyre (the practice known as *suttee*). During the Chinese dynasties, different kinds of human sacrifices would often accompany the death of the emperor. The bottom line is this: if there is no single, universal code of morality assumed to come from the Creator, then, ultimately, every person or society is free to choose or create their own moral system.

---

14. "There must be a law that no imperfect or maimed child shall be brought up, and to avoid an excess of population, some children must be exposed, for a limit must be fixed to the population of the state" (Aristotle, *Politics VII*).

There is no dearth of examples since the dawn of history of where this has occurred. When a person becomes a criminal, or a state commits murder in the name of a political ideology, or a nation founded on democratic principles colonizes and enslaves another people, or an empire sets up a coliseum and pits people against beasts for the entertainment of the masses—in each case, humans have forged their own definitions of what is right and what is wrong.

Furthermore, the moral aspect is always independent of the intelligence, sophistication, and cultural or scientific advancement of a people. Nazi Germany, for example, was one of the most culturally and scientifically advanced nations in the world, yet it built factories to systematically slaughter human beings. Again, the conclusion is inescapable: either morality is universal and derives from an absolute authority, or the battle between good and evil throughout history has been an illusion.

The special appeal of Judaism lies in its assertion that not only is there one source of morality, but the source—the Creator—has outlined for us, in exceedingly great detail, what the right and wrong codes of conduct are. God fashioned us with infinitely complex needs and desires and placed us in a very intricate world. Rather than merely decreeing, "Do good and avoid evil," the Creator offered us a wonderfully sophisticated "user's manual"—the Torah—to inspire and teach us how to live.

✿ Intercultural Exchange
(A true anecdote)

As I briskly passed the desk of a Chinese co-worker, she stopped me. "Happy Rosh HaShanah!" she exclaimed. I thanked her cordially and was about to resume my step, whereupon she continued, "I know that tomorrow is Rosh HaShanah, but I have no idea what your holiday is about." As I didn't have time to launch into an elaborate discourse on kingship, divine judgment, prayer, et cetera, I simply replied, "Rosh HaShanah is the Jewish New Year. *Rosh* means 'head', *Ha* means 'the', and *Shanah* means 'year'." After looking at me pensively for a long moment, her face lit up, "Aahh, I y'understand...it's the *Year of the Head!*"

4

New Horizons

Camping, especially rugged camping, is one of those experiences that, it seems, one either has a passion for or one doesn't. You can focus on the majestic landscapes, the quiet solitude, the sweet smell of a cool early morning mist hovering over a still lake, the thrill of encountering fascinating wildlife, the unobstructed sunsets, the fun of building a fire and roasting marshmallows under a starry night sky. Or you can choose to focus on the duress of backpacking under the gruelling heat of the sun, the unwanted rainfall and uncomfortably cold nights, the persistent and irritating buzzing and bites of mosquitoes and black flies, the lack of basic amenities such as flush toilets, electricity, and running water, the fear of a bear attacking the tent while you sleep.

Belinda and I belong to the first "camp." There is a park about a five-hour drive northeast of Toronto, called Algonquin Park, which is more than 2,500 square miles in size, with thousands of sparkling lakes, hundreds of species of birds, a few dozen types of mammals, and a thousand species of plants. I told Belinda about this park a few weeks after we met. She was very excited. Although she used to go camping as a child, Hong Kong, she pointed out, was much too small to hold parks of that calibre; Hong Kong, for that matter, could probably *fit* inside such a park. We packed clothes, food, tents, first aid supplies, and other camping necessities, got into my silverish-grey Tercel, and headed off on our summer adventure. We rented a canoe. Armed with map and compass, we paddled along a maze of narrow waterways, swam in wide freshwater lakes, and portaged our way to an island campsite as deep in the park's interior as we could get to in the few days that we had. We encountered a moose, a beaver, foxes, loons taking off and landing on the lake, water snakes swimming right by us, and colourful birds and wildflowers. We tried as much as possible not to disturb the flora and fauna and to minimize our impact on the precious and delicate environment. In the evenings we walked, hand in hand, under crisp night skies, listening to the strange and mysterious sounds of the wildlife, breathing in the solitude, and occasionally being entertained by the dance of fireflies illuminating the darkness around us.

When one is immersed in nature like this, I remember thinking, who needs religion? Ever since I was a child, the times I was able to most easily connect to God were when I was close to nature.

One early fall evening, Belinda and I were driving some-where in the city when, through the upper left corner of our windshield, a breathtaking view caught our attention. The moon was full and unusually big against a patch of clear sky. It was vivid, intense, and appeared much closer to earth than it should have. We could even make out rough contours on its surface. It had a magnificent yellowish-orange hue. We quickly stopped the car and got out. We spent a few minutes staring at this unexpected gift of nature. I suggested that we go to my apartment to get my binoculars, convinced that it would enable us to see inside the larger craters. As we started driving, it occurred to Belinda that by the time we arrived home, the sky would almost certainly change. What to do? While lamenting the prospect of missing out on a unique opportunity to "get the most out of life," a brilliant idea occurred to me. We were near a mall. I explained my plan to Belinda and, after some hesitation, she consented.

We walked briskly into an electronics store, spotted a pair of binoculars under the glass countertop, quickly fired a few questions at the store owner, and minutes later found ourselves back in the parking lot of the mall with a newly purchased pair of binoculars. By this time the moon had become considerably smaller and lost much of its lustre. After some fifteen minutes of admiring the moon (now rapidly fading) through the extra pair of lenses, we walked back to the store and returned the binoculars for a full refund. In our haste to buy them, I explained, we realized upon opening the box that they were not the kind we wanted.

We often recalled this incident. Initially we consoled ourselves that we had done nothing wrong. After all, it was legal. I regretted that instead of continuing to enjoy the moon with our naked eyes, we made a tactical mistake of wasting precious time in securing binoculars. Over time, as we became more steeped in Judaism, we gained greater awareness of the unethical nature of our conduct and felt deep remorse and disbelief that we actually had done such a thing.

Judaism trains us to be sensitive to others. According to Judaism, it is forbidden even to ask a storeowner the price of merchandise that one clearly has no intention of buying. This does not refer to comparison shopping, which is legitimate. An example would be a man of little financial means walking into a fine jewellery store in a three-piece suit, pretending to be interested in making a purchase, and asking prices of various expensive items. Unbeknown to the storeowner, his agenda is pure curiosity; he has no money and no intention of making a purchase. Such behaviour raises the store owner's hopes and expectations, not to mention wasting his or her time. The prohibition is but one of numerous examples wherein Jewish law cultivates a sensitivity toward others that prevents the pursuit of selfish interests at others' expense.

Love of nature, without an objective moral guide, can lead to selfishness.

The following summer Belinda and I looked forward with great excitement to a return trip to Algonquin Park. There had been increasing tension between us over the issue of our religious backgrounds, as we delved deeper and deeper into our religious studies. I felt that we both needed some respite. Over the past few months I had been raising the issue of religion frequently, even suggesting to Belinda that she pursue a course on Judaism. If we were to make any headway in resolving "our dilemma," I kept telling her, the more we understood each other's background the more chance we had to succeed. For her part, Belinda resented that I kept subtly and persistently pressuring her to take such a course. She was interested in learning about Judaism, but wanted to do it on her own terms. She hated that our relationship seemed increasingly, from my perspective, to hinge on it.

The weeks leading up to our trip were filled with great anticipation. I purchased new camping supplies from a specialty store. I spent a lot of time drawing up and revising lists of what to bring; studying the map of Algonquin Park, including its lakes, hiking trails, and canoe routes; and exercising at the gym. I wanted this trip to be even better than the first. I borrowed two small books from the library on adventure camping, which I planned to delve into during our stay at the campsite. Against my instinct, I made a conscious decision not to take along any books on Judaism or religion and promised myself that during the four days of our trip I would not initiate any discussion on these subjects.

On the first day we were busy. We drove to the park, registered with the park authorities, loaded and launched a canoe, stopped to eat, headed back onto the waters, and eventually reached our first campsite. We were exhausted. We had been very task-focused the entire day. Since Belinda was more adept than I in a number of camping skills, at times I felt as though I needed to prove my superiority. Occasionally, it felt like we were competing rather than cooperating on tasks.

We got up late the next day. After breakfast Belinda went for a solo ride in the canoe while I chose to sit by the lake and read the books I had brought. My goal was to get as absorbed in nature and adventure camping as I could. It didn't work. I was not completely at peace with myself. I had begun interacting with Belinda as a friend rather than as her "boyfriend." Externally, I was just as friendly and considerate toward her, but for some reason there was a lack of *feeling*. After some thought, I attributed this to the fact that I had high expectations for our trip, based on the previous year's fabulous experience. I told myself that I should focus on the present. Although it might lack the novelty of the previous trip, this time could be just as wonderful in its own way.

Shortly after Belinda returned from the lake, I passed by her tent and saw her profile inside. "Is everything okay?" She did not respond. I stepped inside and found her lying on her stomach with her face buried in the sleeping mat. I heard her muffled whimpers. I gently rubbed her back and asked what was wrong. "Nothing." I asked again, and yet again. Eventually she lifted her head and told me, in a saddened voice, that she felt I was "distant" from her.

I was confused. "What gave you the impression I am distant from you?" I asked lovingly. She couldn't tell me. She said that in the past two days she just felt at times, from the way

I spoke to her, that there was a lack of connection between us. She could not explain it.

After a few minutes it dawned on me that the cause of this "distance" was probably the promise I had secretly made to myself. Our pursuit of clarity about life, our longing to grow spiritually, and our desire to face the challenges in our relationship had underpinned all our interactions since the first day we met. To suddenly and artificially suspend all this, especially without letting Belinda know my intention, was to appear as a different "Yankl." After discussing this matter at some length, our feeling of closeness was rekindled.

That evening we both realized that it was exactly one year since we had met.

"They Live as if God is Real"

With more than 160,000 Jews, Toronto in the 1990s boasted the largest Jewish population in Canada, claiming the title from Montreal in the previous decade. This was due largely to a mass influx of young Jews from Montreal who sought to escape the tense and uncertain political climate in the province of Quebec, generated by wrangling over French language and sovereignty issues.

The observant Jewish population of Toronto in the '90s was growing rapidly and continued to expand northward. New kosher restaurants were springing up, along with food stores, bakeries, specialty shops, agencies, schools, and cultural institutions. A daily Jewish radio program was launched.

A month after we met, I had taken Belinda to a Reform synagogue. She commented that it felt like a Catholic church. We attended several Reform social events, including a Shabbos hike in the woods, as well as classes on various spiritual topics. I surmised that Reform, being the most liberal Jewish system, would be more accepting of my relationship with a non-Jew than the other denominations, and that Belinda might feel relatively comfortable in such an environment. Indeed, we found the people friendly and non-judgmental, and we enjoyed the events.

It was precisely because Reform was so accepting of my rela-tionship with Belinda that very soon I felt a need to venture into the Conservative and Orthodox camps. I wanted our relationship to be approved among the widest spectrum of Jewish people, and if we couldn't gain acceptance from the more traditional elements, I wanted to understand why.

At this point, Orthodoxy impressed me as rigid and obsessive. I was not ready to expose us to such an "extreme" mindset. We found ourselves affiliated with the Conservative move-ment by default. Besides attending a few lectures and events, we befriended a wonderful couple, Linda and Larry, who invited us repeatedly for Shabbos and Jewish holidays. Apart from their generous hospitality, they are among the most spiritual and Jewishly passionate people that Belinda and I have met to this day. One festival that particularly captivated us was *Sukkos*, a special time each autumn when Jews leave the security of their homes and dwell in family-sized huts. Surrounding themselves with minimal material needs, they contemplate the fragility of everything physical and delight in the awareness that the Creator oversees and protects. I remember sitting in Linda and Larry's beautifully adorned *sukkah* (hut), enjoying a sumptuous vegetarian supper, chanting uplifting Hebrew and Yiddish songs, and gazing at the night stars through apertures in the makeshift roof. Although I had been in our oversized synagogue sukkah many times growing up, squeezed in with dozens of other congregants (standing room only, please), this was the first time I felt I had *dwelled* in one. It was intimate. Belinda said it reminded her of camping.

All three major denominations of Judaism — Reform, Conservative and Orthodox — officially oppose intermarriage.[15] However, with regard to interdating, if I could use the term "laissez-faire" to sum up my perception of the Reform position, I would employ "ambivalent" to describe that of the Conservative movement. Only in Orthodoxy did I sense a consistent and definitive stance: interdating is wrong.

In the spring of 1995 I moved into the "vertical *shtetl*". This high-rise, at the corner of Shelborne Avenue and Bathurst Street, had the highest concentration of observant Jewish tenants anywhere in the city. Though happy to be living there, I was not eager to get to know my religious neighbours, and I kept mostly to myself. I did not want to socialize and risk inadvertently becoming one of *them*. However, my thirst for learning was overwhelming and I enthusiastically sought out classes and lectures in and around the neighbourhood, often inviting Belinda along.

15. While Reform Judaism discourages intermarriage, the movement is divided on whether rabbis should officiate at such interfaith weddings when the couple is determined to get married anyway.

We spent many *Shabbosim*[16] and Jewish holidays with a Hassidic family that an out-of-town friend had introduced me to. They were of very modest means, but lived spiritually rich and meaningful lives. We always had lively and deep discussions over delectable food in their small apartment, and we learned a lot about the Jewish religious worldview. Occasionally, we would delve into fascinating elements of the mystical tradition, which made me realize how much more there was to Judaism than I had ever imagined. I was really impressed that, on the one hand, they lived in such an ethereal headspace, while at the same time they were very grounded and concerned with the most minute details of their interaction with the physical world.

More than simply imparting knowledge, this couple and their small child were role models of ethical and joyful living and a tremendous inspiration for our growth in Judaism.

Over time, we were invited for Shabbos meals by other families too, occasionally also to sleep over. Belinda felt uneasy about this. She considered it awkward to stay overnight with total strangers. Soon, however, she became more comfortable with the idea as we blended ever more into the Orthodox Jewish community.

Orthodox Jews seemed to take their religion very seriously and to practice it scrupulously. They didn't just lead "spiritual" lives. God was very much present and had specific and tangible demands to which they diligently attended. We

---

16. The plural form of Shabbos. Also, *Shabbatot*.

had not gotten the same sense from the Conservative or Reform Jews.

"I feel that the Orthodox live as if God is *real*," Belinda remarked to me one day.

※

That fall I sought the counsel of a Reform rabbi. I was especially interested in discussing my situation with a female rabbi, figuring a woman would be better able to see things from my girlfriend's point of view, empathize with her plight, and offer advice that would be respectful of her situation. To terminate a growing relationship with Belinda merely because she was not Jewish, as Rabbi Silver had urged me to do, seemed heartless, no matter how gently or tactfully it was done.

I called the temple office and asked to discuss an "important and delicate personal issue" with Rabbi Zimmerman at her earliest convenience. She was young and dynamic. I knew of her from a lecture she had given. I debated whether to wear a kippa, out of respect for a rabbi, and finally decided not to.

She greeted me warmly, extending her hand. As we sat down in her office, I couldn't help thinking how different it would be if she were a traditional rabbi. Not only would she not extend her hand to a man, she wouldn't even be a woman. (There were no female Orthodox rabbis.)

We were seated facing each other in a closed room, with no furniture between us. I felt uncomfortable, as I had become conscious of the laws of *tsnius,* or modesty, which impose specific restrictions on the kinds of privacy that men and women who are not closely related may share.

"Rabbi Zimmerman, I came to seek your advice on whether to terminate my relationship with my girlfriend, who is a gentile."

"Why isn't she here with you?"

"I didn't want to put extra pressure on her. In fact, she doesn't even know about this meeting."

"I see." She nodded supportively.

As I drew out my tale she passed a box of tissues toward me, and I was embarrassed to make use of it to wipe my tears. I was relieved when it was finally her turn to talk.

"Your pain and anguish stem from the fact that you have chosen to immerse yourself in an Orthodox environment, which does not tolerate interdating and promotes rigid thinking," came the diagnosis.

"Your situation, as you described it, is cause for joy, not anguish," the rabbi continued. "It is very difficult to find a truly compatible soul mate, where each partner truly respects and loves the other. You and Belinda are most fortunate to have found each other."

The prognosis was even favourable: "As for the fact that she is not Jewish—not to worry. Consider inviting her to the classes and activities of the temple, and exposing her to the beauty of Reform Judaism."

I wished it were that easy, I thought. Although Belinda undoubtedly had been enjoying her exposure to Judaism more and more, she had also become increasingly suspicious and resentful of my pressuring her to speed up her learning. Inviting her to another synagogue would further raise the tension between us, and it would be my fault were that to happen.

"What if she would not want to go?" I asked, trying not to sound offensive.

"From what you have been telling me, she is open to learning about Judaism, isn't she?"

"That's true...I guess what I'm wondering is, how long should I give her to decide whether she wants to become Jewish?"

The rabbi smiled. "There is no set time frame; each person is different. You should look at things positively; things will work out if they are meant to, and if not, it is because they were not meant to. You need to have *emunah* (trust in God). In the meantime, everything you described seems so wonderful!"

"But what about the fact that I want a lot of kids, and Belinda is pushing thirty?"

"She's still young; many couples today have their first child in their mid-thirties or even late thirties. Besides, in the worst case, you could adopt."

And so our conversation went. A very sympathetic rabbi who offered me words of encouragement and reassurance. It was what my heart needed to hear, but my soul sought deeper answers.

※

Early that winter Belinda and I broke up. The tension between us had become unbearable. I was at her place. "Do we *always* have to talk about religion?" she exclaimed with biting acerbity, before running to her room, diving onto her bed, and breaking into tears.

I tried to talk to her, to comfort her, but nothing helped. She handed me my extra car key and we agreed to return each other's belongings in the coming days. We looked at each other with tear-filled eyes. After some hesitation, we decided to hug for the last time. The next morning I called in sick. Belinda went to work.

Two days later she called to ask if she could see me. In my mind, I had already terminated the relationship and was "in mourning." My heart, remote and numb, began to stir with a tinge of hope. Nonchalantly, I responded that if she wanted to come over, she was welcome. She did, and we talked at length, while holding hands. She said she was willing to continue to try to work things out. We resumed our relationship.

※

One evening, during a leisurely walk, I brought up the subject of anti-Semitism. It was an easy way, I thought, to get my girlfriend intrigued enough about the Jewish people to investigate Judaism more ambitiously. Having seen *Schindler's List* and visited the Holocaust museum, Belinda knew by now that anti-Semitism meant hatred of Jews, that there had been a long history of Jewish persecutions, and that anti-Semitism reached its most horrible expression in the Holocaust.

"It's actually similar to the Japanese cruelty against the Chinese people during the Second World War," Belinda remarked.

"I can't say I know much about it," I admitted. I wished she had not made such a comparison.

"Well, the Japanese invaded cities and villages, captured and tortured innocent Chinese civilians — "

"Civilians?" I echoed abruptly, as if catching her on a basic factual error.

"Yeah, even those who surrendered. Especially in Nanking. Women as well as young girls were gang-raped by groups of soldiers repeatedly. It's disgusting. In some cases, they even poked long sticks into the ladies just for fun. It's sick. They were animals. With the men, they dug large pits, gathered them around, shot them or chopped their heads off, then let the bodies drop into the pits. They murdered tens of thousands of people within days! I am beyond words to describe what I feel about those soldiers and what they did."

"That's awful," I offered, not sympathetically enough. "What happened to your family?"

"My grandparents fled their home and sought safe haven in Hong Kong."

"Thank God for that. Umm...back to the subject of anti-Semitism...I just want you to be aware and prepared: should you ever become Jewish, your future children will likely be persecuted, and if not, then certainly your grandchildren," I spoke with trepidation. "That in our generation, in prosperous North America, Jews enjoy safety, comfort, and unprecedented freedom among gentiles is an historical anomaly. You can't count on it lasting too long."

Belinda appeared startled.

"Anti-Semitism," I continued slowly, "is the most entrenched, universal, and enduring hatred in history. Unlike the Chinese at the hands of the Japanese, Black slavery in America, or any other national, racial, or ethnic persecution that ever transpired, anti-Semitism is a phenomenon that has eluded all attempts at sociological explanation. Jews have lived in dozens of countries and been expelled from quite a number of them. From ancient times to modern times, throughout Christian Europe and in the Muslim world, whether by socialists or fascists, whether at the hands of pagans, secular societies, or religious communities, Jews have been despised and persecuted."

Belinda thought I was exaggerating. She was starting to get annoyed by my diatribe. She felt Jews were paranoid, thinking everyone was out to get them. I reiterated, like a broken record, that anti-Semitism was unique and inexplicable.

Privately, though, I wondered if she wasn't right. Having been raised on the idea that we are the "Chosen People," was it not normal to think that everyone else would be envious and hold us in contempt? Perhaps we have even wished some of the scorn upon ourselves. I recalled a sympathetic army chaplain who confided in me when I joined the Canadian reserves as a teenager: "I have often wondered, are the Jews hated because they are different, or are they different because they are hated?"

"I think it's both," I replied, somewhat unsure.

It's Not About Tradition

In April 1996 we drove to Hamilton, about an hour's drive from Toronto, to spend the first Passover Seder at Linda's parents. As we had at Linda and Larry's, we felt extremely welcome. We feasted on rich readings, delectable discussions, and spiced-up singing as family members and guests joined together in reawakening the drama of the Exodus. We returned home very late that evening, with satisfied souls and stomachs, a bit overwhelmed by the experience.

I had arranged to do the second Seder at my place the following evening, inviting just Belinda. It was the first time I would attempt to conduct a Seder, but I was quite confident, having observed my father do it year after year. All the ritual paraphernalia were laid out: matzos, wine, hard-boiled egg, bitter herb, green vegetable, shank bone, salt water, and the *Hagaddah*. And, of course, I had prepared an elaborate meal.

As it turned out, Belinda was delayed at work. Being a senior technical support analyst for the company, she not uncommonly had to work overtime to "fire-fight" when there were problems.

In the course of the late afternoon and into the evening Belinda called to update me on her tardiness, each time with an apology and reassurance that she would be held up just a bit longer.

I was getting more impatient with each call. Didn't she understand the significance and importance of the Passover Seder? Didn't she realize how much planning and preparation went in, having been to one the previous evening? Couldn't she tell her boss she had an important commitment?

I tried to conceal my frustration. I didn't want her to come into the Seder with a sour taste, to associate the Passover experience with rushing and unpleasantness.

I was becoming increasingly hungry.

When the phone rang again, I let the answering machine pick it up. I didn't want to risk speaking to her in an angry voice, and anyway there was nothing I could do. I listened hopefully as she left a message that she was on her way.

While waiting for Belinda to arrive (it was already very late), I flipped through the pages of the Hagaddah trying to decide how to truncate the Seder: which parts could be omitted and which I would skim over quickly, in the interest of getting to the meal.

This got me thinking. Why are certain parts of the Hagaddah so significant? How does one weigh one's hunger pangs against the importance of going through particular rituals? What does it all ultimately mean? Was the Seder important mainly because it was an entrenched family tradition? What about now that my family was hundreds of miles away?

I had always been under the impression that Passover was a remembrance of God freeing the Israelites from slavery in Egypt and a celebration of our freedom. In fact, many Jewish holidays, such as Hanukkah or Purim, are, superficially, occasions to celebrate our victory over enemies who tried to oppress or kill us thousands of years ago. (As someone wryly summed it up: "They tried to kill us. We won. Let's eat.") What was the big deal about marking these events? What relevance did it have for my life today? What relevance did this have to Belinda's life?

It would be months later that we would learn that Passover, and indeed all the Jewish holidays, are not about the past as much as they are about the present: that is, each holiday brings a unique spiritual energy and set of moral lessons aimed at transforming us into more sensitive and ethical human beings. Passover has to do with the meaning of freedom in our lives today. Hanukkah is more about overcoming current assimilationist tendencies than about glorifying some ancient military victory. Purim aims to cultivate a profound awareness that all occurrences today, including the most seemingly mundane ones, are divinely orchestrated, albeit in a concealed manner.

In fact, all Jewish holidays are God-centric. Without God in the picture, it seemed to me, there was ultimately no reason why we should eat matzos, why we should light the Hanukkah menorah, or why we should *shlep* to synagogue and listen to the reading of the Megillah—especially when such rituals inconvenience us.

Without God, there was no compelling reason why we couldn't postpone our Passover Seder from Thursday evening to the weekend, when Belinda and I would be off work and more relaxed. Tradition, no matter how entrenched, did not seem to be a persuasive enough argument to justify my hunger pangs.

Deuteronomy 7:1–5

Not long after, the following entry appeared in my diary:

I went to work today, as usual. A very boring day, uneventful. I was feeling somewhat depressed. Last night I was at Belinda's house. She cried all evening. It wasn't the first time she cried so much; it's been a common occurrence in our relationship.

Last Shabbat we drove (!) to Thornhill to hear Rabbi Burowitz (our favourite lecturer) talk about the relationship that Jews should have to the non-Jewish world. We learned that, according to Deuteronomy, a Jew must not marry a non-Jew.[17] We had learned a few months earlier that the Torah prohibited intermarriage, but now we learned the actual source. This had a powerful impact on Belinda. She went home that evening and looked up the source in the *khumash*[18] and studied the commentaries.

Belinda has been depressed all week. She feels that the Torah might be true. For the first time, she tells me, she feels that the Jewish people are very important for the world. She is concerned about Jewish continuity! She feels it is wrong for me to be dating her, as she is not Jewish, and that I should perhaps return to my people and carry on the unique Jewish mission.

I explained to her that she has been a catalyst in my returning to Judaism.

Belinda is confused. She is very serious about the question of conversion: she absolutely refuses to convert for the sake of marriage; she likes the teachings of Orthodox Judaism a lot and might want to convert; she does not know if she would be capable

17. "When the Lord your God brings you to the land that you will inherit, many nations will fall away before you...And you shall not marry with them; do not give your daughter to his son and do not take his daughter for your son. For he will turn your son away from Me and they will worship other gods..." (Deuteronomy 7:1–5)
18. The Five Books of Moses. The Written Torah.

of being an observant Jew, as Judaism's rituals are "so alien" to her and its lifestyle so demanding; and she really, really wants to be sure — if she does choose to convert — that it is not because of our relationship. Also, she wonders if the decision to convert may even come in ten years? And how long can we wait? She is also very depressed about the possibility of losing me. For my part, I told Belinda that: 1) I admire her high integrity; 2) becoming Jewish is a gradual, lengthy process; 3) I am not looking to marry an Orthodox Jew, although Orthodoxy seems to be the direction in which I am heading; 4) I love Belinda very much; 5) I want to marry someone who is a convert or a *baalas teshuvah*,[19] as opposed to someone born religious. The former can appreciate Judaism more, in many cases.[20] Also, one reason I am attracted to Belinda is that I want to be able to keep in touch with the world, and not be insular...

During the next few weeks, Belinda's weeping was often interminable. I would look at her grief and howl within my own soul. I wished I could say something — anything — to stop the tears. Whatever consolation I attempted invariably had the opposite effect, so that in the end I would sit close to her in utter helplessness, hold her hand, and wonder why God fashioned human eyes with a capacity for manufacturing an infinite supply of salt water.

19. A previously non-observant Jewish woman who has "returned" to her heritage.

20. I perceived Jews who had grown up in an observant environment as being very susceptible to living their religious life mechanically.

"Don't cry so much; it hurts me too!" I wanted to scream. "Besides, there is so much that you and I still don't know and have yet to understand about our theological dilemma, about Judaism, about what God does or does not want."

Sometimes the situation became alarming. Belinda would complain of acute pain in her chest (close to her heart, she'd say) even if she wasn't crying at all but merely *thinking* about our situation. It was the first time in her life that emotional distress directly produced real physical pain, something I had not thought possible.

Belinda tended to see the world more in black and white than I did. Sometimes this drove me crazy, and she'd express similar frustrations about my ambivalences. In the world of ideas, I was more adept at living with ambiguity. This is reflected in our different career paths. She is technically oriented; I am the social work type. Her career is computers; mine is helping needy people. She attained A's in almost all her courses from junior high through college. I had no problem failing some courses I'd lost interest in, and did not let that affect my self-esteem as I moved on to undergraduate and then graduate studies.

One evening the pain was so severe that I wanted to drive her to the hospital. Because she refused, we went for a ride.

"Where are you taking us?" she muttered, breaking the heavy silence.

"You'll see." I deliberately created an aura of mystery and suspense.

After fifteen minutes I stopped the car. We were in front of a middle-class bungalow in a Jewish neighbourhood. I had rented the basement of that house before I met Belinda. We sat in the car as I talked about Mr. and Mrs. Kramer.

"They are of my father's generation, also from Eastern Europe. On many Saturdays the couple would invite me upstairs for a light lunch."

"That's very kind of them...They keep Shabbos?"

"They're not strictly observant — I'd say ninety percent. They keep a kosher kitchen. We'd speak in Yiddish, which further bonded us and made them feel like I was their own son. We'd sing Yiddish songs at the table."

"What did you talk about?"

"Everything. But the husband would take pleasure in recounting his tribulations in an anti-Semitic society, both in Europe before the war, and later when he came to America. He'd slip into these personal anecdotes very easily. Often his stories tried to show how Jewish values and sensibilities were *superior* to those of non-Jews. It's almost as if he wanted to teach me something."

"I see. What did you learn from him?"

"I don't know. I felt uncomfortable hearing some of the stories. Sometimes I tried to change the subject."

"I see."

"They're extremely nice and warm people. They always introduced me to their friends as a guest—*never* as a tenant. They gave me a very good deal on the rent, too."

"Is that why you didn't question him on his views?"

"Actually, sometimes I did, but this would agitate him. I wanted to show consideration. They were Holocaust survivors. They went through hell. A quiet, principled couple. I think his world would have been even more unreachable had we not both spoken Yiddish."

"Did they ever push observance on you?"

"Never, except that sometimes the husband would invite me to join him at his Orthodox synagogue—which I always declined."

My purpose in taking Belinda to this house (we did not go inside) was to distract her from her thoughts, and provide temporary relief from her pain. It worked, though I wondered when the next emotional crisis would erupt.

The Noahide Laws

Belinda and I arrived unusually early in the rapidly filling, large synagogue auditorium where J. David Davis, a former southern U.S. Baptist minister, was scheduled to speak. It was Sunday, April 28. Under intense Jewish media coverage and amid a buzz of audience excitement, he shared the story of how he, together with his Baptist congregation, had begun to investigate the roots of the Christian faith a number of years earlier. His unrelenting search for Truth eventually led him to an Orthodox rabbi, where he learned of one of the most fundamental, yet obscure, doctrines of biblical tradition: the Seven Universal Laws of Noah. Since then, Davis's Baptist temple had been transformed into a centre of learning and educational dissemination for the Noahide movement. The activities of this Baptist minister and his community caused a local furor, which led to local and international media coverage, including a front-page story in the *Wall Street Journal* and an appearance on the *Larry King show.*

What are the Seven Universal Laws of Noah? According to the Bible, when God created humanity there was no division into Jews and gentiles. This would not happen for at least twenty generations, when Abraham, the first Jew, would appear on the scene. Under what moral code were people expected to live before Abraham and before the Torah was given to the Jewish nation at Mount Sinai? According to our Oral Tradition, several broad categories of laws were given to Adam and later to Noah (after the Flood), which were binding on all their descendants — in other words, all mankind. These laws are the foundation of Western ethical and moral values.

As Davis's organization points out, the Noahide religion is the oldest one in the world. On March 20, 1991, United States President George Bush signed into law a historic joint resolution of both Houses of Congress that, among other things, recognizes the Seven Noahide Laws as the "bedrock of society from the dawn of civilization" and urges the United States to "return the world to the moral and ethical values contained in the Seven Noahide Laws." The resolution recognizes that "without these ethical values and principles the edifice of civilization stands in serious peril of returning to chaos."[21]

The seven categories of laws, as expounded in the Jewish Oral Tradition, are 1) the prohibition against murder and suicide; 2) the prohibition against idolatry — the worship of any human or object — and prohibition against involvement with the occult; 3) the prohibition against wrongly taking another's goods or property; 4) the prohibition against illicit sexual relations; 5) the prohibition against eating flesh cut from a living animal and the imperative to treat animals kindly; 6) the prohibition against any blasphemy or curse against the Creator; and 7) the imperative to establish courts of law to implement the six other laws and pursue social justice. Within each of these categories are numerous ordinances and ethical norms.

According to Judaism, any gentile who accepts and lives by the Universal Laws of Noah is righteous and has a share in the World-to-Come. Because of persecution of the Jews, little has been done to teach these laws for the past few thousand years. Interest in them has revived in recent years, and Noahide groups and literature have started up around the world.

According to Davis, most Noahides have turned away from some of the standard holidays of the West, such as Christmas and Easter with their pagan associations. To be a Noahide, no formal religious ritual or liturgy is required, although shared traditions and texts and meeting together for prayer and study

21. H.J. Res. 104, Public Law 102–14.

is considered necessary to build a viable Noahide society. More and more, Noahides are involved in cooperation with leading rabbis in Israel, the United States, and elsewhere, in developing prayers, ceremonies, and rituals that are appropriate to them. Within the constraints of the Noahide laws, there is ample opportunity for diverse spiritual approaches and practices.

Belinda and I had heard about the Universal Laws of Noah prior to attending this talk. What intrigued us was to actually meet a Noahide and learn the extent and strength of the Noahide community worldwide. Belinda was particularly curious about the viability of leading a full and meaningful religious life as a Noahide as an alternative to converting to Judaism.

I returned home disconcerted. At some level I had assumed that, no matter how demanding Judaism was, my strong-headed girlfriend would ultimately want to become Jewish should she ever conclude that it was grounded in truth. I had not reckoned on the bizarre possibility that a religion (in this case, Judaism) could be true and at the same time exempt most people (the gentiles) from living by most of its laws and precepts.

As it was, Belinda was not impressed with the size of the Noahide community. For now, she would let the Noahide option simmer in the back of her mind.

5

Acquiring Clarity

*Once, while sitting and listening to a Jewish lecture,
Belinda felt very angry and "cheated." She grew up in
Hong Kong and was never exposed to such ideas. She was
astounded that such a tiny group of people — the Jews —
had so much wisdom and kept it all to themselves!*

*E*arlier that year Belinda had learned, through the
Village Shul, about a month-long summer learning
and touring experience in Israel for young people. The
entire program was heavily subsidized by private individuals
in the community. Participants were responsible for airfare,
but everything else (lodging, food, touring, and so on) was
sponsored.

When Belinda told me that she would be interested in applying, I expressed mild delight while privately, in my imagination, I burst into joyful Hassidic dance. We both applied. The application required submitting one's latest academic grades and composing an essay on two themes: Why do you want to go on the trip? What are the most important things you want to have accomplished by the end of your life? A personal interview was not necessary, as the rabbi in charge of the selection knew us well.

Belinda's academic achievements were impressive and her essay reflected a genuine interest in learning more about Judaism and growing as a person. We were both accepted into the program.

However, because she was not Jewish, her special case was discussed by the program committee. Their decision was that as long as other Jewish candidates were interested, her spot would have to be yielded.

As it turned out, the quota of twenty-five Jewish women (there was a separate quota of twenty-five men) was filled, and it became clear that she would not be going. At the last minute, however, one woman cancelled, and this opened the way for Belinda to go. We were elated.

Belinda had never been to Israel, and she was nervous about going because of the violence that so often appeared on the television news. In the months leading up to the summer trip, there had been a particularly sharp increase in terrorist activity.

We found out later that because Belinda was not Jewish she was ineligible for any subsidies and would have to pay the entire cost of the trip herself, a situation that placed her in a financial predicament.

Belinda knew that I would have cancelled my own participation, on principle, had she not been accepted because she was not Jewish. However, I kept from her the fact that, as she *was* now approved, I was prepared to go on the trip even if she were to decline.

Despite the obstacles, Belinda eventually decided to go, although it was a close call. And fortuitous: the Jerusalem Fellowship Program would take me a long way toward my passionately embracing Judaism. Were Belinda not to participate in the program, it is possible that our relationship might have ended after my return to Canada.

Experiencing the Holy Land

"Who is wise? One who learns from every person...Who is strong? One who is able to control one's personal desires...Who is rich? One who is happy with one's lot."[22]

Seated comfortably in a classroom overlooking the Western Wall, we listened attentively as the rabbi illuminated the Torah's approach to living. I had been to Israel several times before, but this was my first trip in a purely religious

22. Chapters of the Sages 4:1.

117

Kotel (the Western Wall), Jerusalem

context. It was June 1996. We were met with an intensive schedule of classes and seminars on such diverse topics as the uniqueness and wonders of Jewish history, science and religion, the purpose of the Torah, sexuality, free will, prayer, levels of happiness, current Middle East politics, Jewish legal philosophy, and the afterlife. There was an optional class on intermarriage, which Belinda decided to skip, fearing it would be too emotional for her and worrying that her visible non-Jewish presence might inhibit honest dialogue among participants.

Interspersed with these classes were fun-filled activities including hallah-baking,[23] Israeli folk dancing for women,

23. Hallah is a special kind of bread used for Shabbos and holidays.

various sports, and a tour of the Christian and Muslim quarters of the Old City. More adventurous events included a trip to Safed, an ancient city infused with a mystical tradition. We also visited a winery in northern Israel, climbed the hundreds of steps leading to the famous historical fortress at Masada, floated on the Dead Sea, rappelled down rocky hills, stepped inside the Flour Caves (white caves with an unusual, chalk-like texture), kayaked along the Jordan river, stumbled through some dark, wet ancient tunnel, and explored the very Orthodox neighbourhood of Meah Shearim.

No religious observances were required from participants. We were only requested to be respectful of the observance of others and adhere to certain standards of modesty in dress.

Shabbos was ethereal, especially in the Old City. We were matched with host families, who delighted in sharing with us their stories and songs. Shabbos was the high point of the week for the whole community, and this was felt even in the street. The evening air was warm and pleasant. Time stood still. We prayed by the Western Wall — a remnant of the ancient Temple, the focal point of God's manifestation in the world, which, Jews believe, will be rebuilt once we merit it.

I thought of my *Bar Mitzvah*[24] eighteen years earlier. It had taken place right there, in the exact spot where I was standing.

---

24. A public ceremony held around a Jewish boy's thirteenth birthday (technically, his entry into his fourteenth year) to mark the fact that he is henceforth obligated in all Torah observances. Although most secular Jews have a Bar Mitzvah and view it as an important rite of passage, most do not take the obligation aspect seriously.

Many things were the same: the dry, still air; the yellowish-grey stones; the partition between the men's and women's sections; a few chairs; a podium in the middle. Missing was the intense afternoon sun, the crowd, the commotion, the throngs of my father's friends and some relatives — most of whom I did not even know — who had come from near and far to be part of my special day.

I relived standing at the podium and reading from the Torah scroll, not understanding what I was reading and being afraid to make mistakes. I remembered, as if it were yesterday, the merriment of singing and dancing with my parents, brothers, uncles, and cousins around the Torah. I recalled the candies that were thrown at me from the women's section, the exuberant cheering and cries of "Mazal Tov!", the hugs and kisses and attention and gifts that were showered upon me — for doing what? Turning thirteen?

Belinda and I found the classes and seminars intellectually stimulating and eye-opening. We were welcome — indeed, encouraged — to express our views and fire challenging questions at the rabbis both inside and outside the classroom. The atmosphere during the month-long program was charged with camaraderie. Participants bonded. People grew and changed. I felt that the Jerusalem Fellowship Program was an opportunity to find the most sensible direction for a meaningful life.

Men and women were accommodated in separate apartment complexes. Many classes were separate, as were all weekend and overnight trips. I prayed that Belinda would really enjoy the classes and group experiences, and that they would influence her toward Judaism. I hoped very much that she would be fully accepted by the other participants, despite her Chinese appearance and non-Jewish status, and that she would develop friendships with the women, which would offer her a taste of belonging among the Jewish people.

As it turned out, Belinda befriended many participants. She taught some of them to play Chinese Checkers. During a bus trip, she stood behind the driver and gave a talk to the group about the Chinese Jews of Kaifeng. Belinda connected especially well with Lucy, a pleasant and funny Jewish girl who had herself interdated and was struggling with similar

Learning at the Aish HaTorah Yeshiva in Jerusalem

fundamental religious questions. During free time, I would sometimes catch the two of them taking a walk together. Their friendship has continued to this day.

Sometimes, between classes or activities, Belinda and I spent time alone. We always had a lot to share about our learning and experiences in the program. Once in a while, the conversation drifted to our future. "What if I decide not to convert?" she asked pointedly one time, as we sat outside on a ledge facing the Western Wall.

The question made me uncomfortable. I acknowledged my confusion. I encouraged us to look at the positive side: at least we were growing spiritually; at least we were seeking wisdom and trying to come to terms with whether the Torah was indeed from God. Still, the answer to the perennial question—"What if I decide not to convert?"—eluded me.

I have wonderful aunts, uncles, and cousins in Israel, whom I had not seen in many years. I went to visit them alone. Although I very much wanted Belinda to meet them, I had no idea how accepting they would be of her. I feared that they would try either to dissuade me from continuing the relationship or, worse, pressure her to convert. The more one pushed my girlfriend, I well knew, the more she would resist. God forbid, she might even develop resentment toward Jews.

However, I did arrange to take Belinda to visit my sister and brother, both of whom are observant. My sister lived in Jerusalem and my brother in Netanya. Both were amenable to seeing my girlfriend *once*, but advised me over the phone in no uncertain terms that I must end the relationship.

After spending a few hours with Belinda, my sister commented to me privately that she liked Belinda and would be happy to have a sister-in-law "like her." My brother took an up-front approach. He frankly told Belinda within minutes of being introduced that he did not know her, had nothing against her, but was categorically opposed to our relationship because she wasn't Jewish. As if to underscore this point, he added that if she was interested, he and his wife would be only too happy to have her over for Shabbos some time, as well as me, but not both of us together.

❧

Shortly before the end of the program, I informed the program coordinator that I wished to discuss my situation with a senior rabbi of the Aish HaTorah Yeshiva. He promptly referred me to Rabbi Pomerantz. Despite being overbooked, Rabbi Pomerantz, acknowledging my predicament and imminent return to Canada, managed to create a new, albeit narrow, slot in his calendar.

His face revealed a kind, gentle man. His serene demeanour reflected wisdom accumulated through years of counselling experience. I immediately felt at ease in Rabbi Pomerantz's presence and proceeded to tell my story. I was surprised at how easily my words flowed, how efficiently I was able to convey my complex situation, my hopes and fears, my months of confusion and pent-up frustration. I spoke, uninterrupted, for all but five minutes of my allotted time. The rabbi then asked if I would accompany him as he went about some personal errands, thereby enabling us to talk longer.

As we walked to the bank, the post office, and back to his office, I continued to pour out my heart. I highlighted the fact that Belinda and I were on a quest for truth, but that getting married and starting a family was nonetheless my number one priority in life, and I hated very much the idea of waiting an indefinite length of time for an uncertain outcome. I have the rest of my life to learn and grow, I conveyed to him, but if I hope one day to become a *zeyde* (grandfather), the wheels must be put into motion imminently.

Rabbi Pomerantz said it would be devastating and unwise to break off the relationship with Belinda at this point. However, I should endeavour to change the *nature* of the relationship. Each time we met or otherwise interacted, we should discuss only religious matters and not distract ourselves with other topics or activities. Dating would be circumscribed and highly focused, and any form of physical contact was out of the question. I responded that I would try to follow his advice, while privately I wondered how realistic it was. I then asked him how long I should wait before terminating the relationship. Rabbi Pomerantz thought for a long time. Finally, he replied that if, after one year, she had still not decided that she wanted to become Jewish, then it was safe to assume that she would not become Jewish.

I thanked the rabbi for his time, and did not mention the meeting to Belinda.

Following our return to Toronto, Belinda intensified her Jewish learning. At the same time, she started going to church on Sundays. She went specifically to meet with a Bible teacher who specialized in different religions. One time she invited a speaker to her home to discuss theological issues one on one.

That my girlfriend chose to give Christianity another chance despite her very positive experience in Israel increased my admiration for her truth-seeking zeal. At the same time, however, I lamented the prospect that the resolution of our dilemma would be further delayed.

Kosher Sexuality

Slim, athletic, average height, with a pretty smile and a very cute flat nose. This is how I would describe my girlfriend, at least physically. When I started dating Belinda, my conscience kept telling me that it was wrong for us to have a physical relationship because she was not Jewish — not because we were not married.

During the Jerusalem Fellowship Program, I came across an excellent book, *The Magic Touch*, by Gila Manolson. It deepened my appreciation of the concept of *tsnius*, or modesty, and it helped me to resolve a lot of the confusion I had experienced for years over such issues as premarital relations, kissing in public, "adult" movies and magazines, and the relationship between love and sex. This learning was subsequently enhanced and solidified through further reading, lectures, discussions, and personal reflections.

Here are a few ideas that shaped my new outlook.

The family is the most important determinant of the health of a society. More than any social, educational or religious institution, the close interdependencies and role modeling among family members create the most effective system for transmitting values — positive or negative — to the next generation. Finding a compatible partner and focusing our energies and attention on nurturing the relationship enables us to contribute toward a stable, sane, and functional society.

How do we find a compatible partner? For some, the word "compatibility," in the context of dating, means physical compatibility. Testing such suitability prior to making a long-term commitment is an often-used argument to justify premarital relations. Were this reasoning valid, sexual encounters would need to occur only once or twice before a couple decided either to terminate the relationship (if not sexually compatible) or plan the wedding. The reality is that unmarried couples live together *for years* without making a long-term commitment. And often, once a commitment is finally made, the relationship doesn't last very long. This indicates that there may have been more selfish motives at play all along.

"Chemistry" is very much influenced by trust, emotional bonding, and genuine love. Unless someone is unhealthy or has an obvious physical deformity — which early in the dating process he or she has the moral obligation to disclose — there should be no concern at all about sexual compatibility.

The major problem with premarital relations is that *touch* is a very powerful force, capable of creating an illusion of emotional intimacy and a feeling of commitment that may have no basis in reality. This clouds the intellect and prevents an objective assessment of the other person's character and the suitability of a permanent relationship. Countless couples have tied the knot after blissful experiences in bed only to discover that perfect synchronization in bed did not necessarily transfer to synchronization in dealing with the in-laws, buying a house, resolving inevitable disputes (why the laundry wasn't done), raising children, and so on.

It would seem logical that one of the most important decisions in life — whom to marry — should be made in as level-headed a way and as objectively as possible. This might even include soliciting opinions from trusted family and friends (who, incidentally, do not need to know the prospective partner's abilities in bed). Sadly, in the secular world, such a life-changing decision as marriage is often made in an inebriated state. Our culture even expects that, ultimately, we marry on the basis of "love" or intuition rather than rationality. Judaism views this as risky and irresponsible. In the Orthodox Jewish world one does not marry someone because one has fallen in love with him or her. True love takes time and investment. Rather, one marries based on objective criteria of compatibility (including common interests, values, goals, and temperament) and *then* one learns to love one's new wife or husband through selfless giving, giving without expectation of return. When both spouses are raised with this outlook, their relationship is strong and secure.

In seeking a soul mate, excessive focus on the physical body prevents one from seeing the spiritual side of the person. This is a serious problem in a society that idolizes the female body (and, increasingly, the male body too). An innocuous stroll down a typical commercial street will expose one to enticing images — on magazine covers, in storefronts, on large billboards — of semi-clad women in provocative poses. Although undoubtedly an effective marketing ploy for selling products, it is not without social consequences. For one thing, women are perceived and treated as objects.

In considering a prospective spouse, instead of asking, "Am I the person best able to give to this particular woman what she needs?" the question becomes focused on the self: "Will I get more out of her than I would marrying somebody else?" Rather than seek potential compatibility for mutual growth, men subconsciously assign a "market value" to women (based on a combination of beauty, health, wealth, education, social standing, and so on) and attempt to secure the best deal they can.

Moreover, given the considerable importance of physical appearance, once the "object" is sufficiently depreciated, logic dictates that it be traded in for a replacement: a younger, more beautiful woman. The female spouse must live with the increasing insecurity that she could be discarded because of the effects of aging. Many women do everything they can to keep themselves youthful, attractive, and sexually enticing for fear of finding themselves back in the relationship market, this time as a "used product."

It is worth stating that physical appearance *is* important in choosing a mate. Judaism opposes marrying someone one finds repulsive. If we do not look beyond the level of the physical, however, we miss out on things that are of even greater importance: the person beneath the skin.

Generally speaking, the naked female body is extremely alluring to men, and the male sexual drive is most powerful and difficult to control. When a man is exposed to reasonably attractive, half-clothed women, he is distracted by sexual fantasies. Over the long run, by being repeatedly subjected to such images (on television, at the grocery check-out, at the office, in the bus, or on the street, especially on hot summer days), his sexual sensitivity is dulled, and the capacity to give and receive sexual pleasure from the woman he is committed to is diminished. In my own experience, since I began avoiding shaking hands with and hugging other women, my sensitivity has increased, and when I touch my wife I feel the difference.

When a man casually pecks a woman on the cheek during a business awards ceremony, or a group of friends go camping and guys and girls end up sharing a tent, or a guy dances with a girl at a party, they may think that there is nothing sexually stimulating about what they did. Furthermore, such acts are within the parameters of cultural norms and expectations.

That such activity did not turn them on does not make it right; it makes it *tragic* in that their sexual sensitivities have been dulled. And what a culture sanctions does not make it right or healthy either. There are people, accustomed to frequent one-night stands, who claim that there is nothing wrong with that: a mutually pleasurable act between two consenting adults, with no strings attached. There are also "liberal-minded" couples who agree to exchange spouses for a night to spice up their boring sex lives.

The point is that there are always subcultures, and even the standards and norms of mainstream society are not static. Since the sexual revolution of the '60s, the level of modesty in behaviour and dress in the Western world has declined dramatically. Several years ago, in the province where I live, it became legal for women to go topless in the streets and other public places.[25] The boundaries between the private and the public domain have concurrently eroded, as evidenced by people revealing the most intimate details of their sex lives openly on national television.

Human beings, our sages teach, are created in the image of God and in the image of animals. At every moment the choice is before us of whose image we want to develop. We can live our lives impulsively, eating whenever we are hungry, having sexual encounters whenever, wherever, and with whomever we please. Or we can elevate everything physical toward the spiritual by using it for its intended purpose. Judaism teaches that the way to get the deepest pleasures out of life is to trade-off quantity for quality, immediate gratification

25. As long as it is not for commercial advantage.

for long-term health and happiness, and unencumbered hedonism for disciplined and purposeful living.

Judaism does not view the body as inherently sinful and sex as a necessary concession for the purpose of procreation. On the contrary, Judaism views the sexual experience as one of the most wonderful gifts from the Creator, the primary purpose of which is to help bond and strengthen the relationship between husband and wife. As with any valuable or precious gift, sex must be scrupulously bulwarked to prevent it from being defiled.

Once a man and a woman have committed themselves to each other through marriage, a genuine spiritual bond is created between them. Romantic dinners and moonlight walks and erotic lovemaking will then express and further cement it. Done at the proper time (after the wedding), in the proper place (complete privacy), with the proper person (spouse), and with the proper intention (to give pleasure to the other), the sexual experience becomes nothing less than holy.

Ultimately, the reasons provided for tsnius are, as in any other area of Jewish law, conjecture. Orthodox Judaism does not purport to know the mind of God, only what God wants from us.

For a long time Belinda's sister used to teasingly call us "sticky rice." For a few months Belinda and I chose to limit our physical affection to hugging and handholding. It was very difficult at first, but soon we got used to it. Eventually, we ceased all physical contact. We were no longer sticky rice, and became cold peas.

A Very Special Day

Turning thirty was traumatic. Although I was gainfully employed, I did not have a flourishing career. Although I had a steady girlfriend, I was not married and did not have my own family. Although I had backpacked across Europe and traveled to the Arctic, I had never visited Asia or South America or Africa. I had expected to accomplish more in life by this milestone.

As my birthday fell on a Friday, I decided to celebrate it by preparing my very first Shabbos dinner for Belinda. I purchased wine, hallah, candles, and a new tablecloth. After lighting the candles, I recited the traditional blessings over the wine and over the hallah, all in Hebrew and from memory. I remembered how, growing up, grape juice or wine somehow tasted sweeter after a blessing had been made over it. We took a photo using the self-timer. It was a delightful evening.

After that I hosted a few other Shabbos meals, inviting friends, both Jewish and non-Jewish. I tried to make the meals as kosher as possible and engage my guests in discussion on meaningful subjects.

Over time, and boosted by the Jerusalem Fellowship Program, I deepened my understanding and appreciation of Shabbos tremendously.

"Remember the Sabbath to keep it holy" is the fourth of the Ten Commandments. Shabbos is the holiest day for Jews. That it occurs frequently — every seven days — does not detract from its holiness.

Hosting my very first Shabbos

The idea of Shabbos has spread throughout the world, largely because of Christianity. The seven-day week, which most of the inhabitants of this planet follow, is a reflection of this.

I used to think that Shabbos was "a day of rest." This is misleading. It is true that on Shabbos we refrain from earning a living. However, technically, we are permitted to move heavy furniture from one part of the house to the other or walk up and down a dozen flights of stairs carrying a heavy load. On the other hand, such "work" as jotting down a few words on a piece of paper or pressing an elevator button is strictly prohibited. Moreover, relaxing on the beach or playing golf on Saturday, as important as these activities are for physical and emotional rejuvenation, do not lend themselves to achieving the unique spiritual goals for which Shabbos is intended.

The root of the Hebrew word Shabbos (or Shabbat) is "to cease." From Friday at sundown to Saturday night, we cease our normal weekday activities and bear testimony that God created *everything:* the physical world, the spiritual world, time itself, us, and even our needs. If we do not conclude that major business deal, or reply to that urgent e-mail, the world will still turn. Shabbos puts activities, which are often born of personal insecurities, in proper perspective. It helps remind us that God, not humans, sustains the world.

In six days we are enjoined to be partners with God to improve the physical conditions of our family, community, and ultimately the world. And on the seventh day we subordinate our personal agenda to the divine will, thereby proclaiming God as sovereign.

No matter how difficult our life circumstances are, God intends for us to work to live and not live to work. Shabbos is a time for *being* rather than *doing,* a time to shut out mundane distractions and remember why we are here: ultimately, to strive to become one with our Creator.

How is Shabbos observed? Various rituals are performed, each of which is infused with meaning and helps sanctify the day. There are also thirty-nine categories of activity from which we abstain: harvesting, cooking, making a permanent knot, tearing, writing, making a fire, and others.

On Shabbos, we don't just pay lip service to God's having sovereignty over us: we live in its reality. This consciousness accompanies our every move. Even the most trivial act, such as tying one's shoelaces or opening a bag of chips, must be executed in a manner that does not violate the Shabbos. Indeed, the scope and manner of our interaction with the physical world on Shabbos would appear bizarre to those outside the observant Jewish circle. On Shabbos, we gear our bodies to a different reality while our souls are elevated to the sublime.

Shabbos is to be thoroughly enjoyed. It is a physical and spiritual oasis. The body, in partnership with the soul, indulges in permitted pleasures. We dress in our finest clothes, set out the nicest tablecloth and china, and eat the finest foods. The community gathers for prayer. We invite friends or total strangers to our table, learn together from the wisdom of our sages, and discuss spiritual matters. The restrictions of Shabbos help us focus on the day, but they are never the focus *of* the day.

The warm glow of the Friday-night candles, the delicious smell of freshly baked hallah, the sweet-tasting wine, and the radiant faces of the children and guests around the table as the traditional blessings are chanted, all create an atmosphere of wholesomeness and peace. There is no television, telephone, computers, or mail to distract any member of the household. The family is *truly* together. You have time for anyone who wishes to talk to you, and everyone has time for you.

Throughout the ages, countless Jews have been fired from their jobs, or suffered worse treatment, because they refused to work on Saturday. Judaism beseeches us never to violate Shabbos except to save a life.[26] Shabbos is an eternal sign of the Jews' faith in and allegiance to God.

I used to consider the Shabbos restrictions burdensome and detracting from the pleasure of living freely. I wondered what kind of a heartless being would demand such cumbersome compliance. Later, as I learned to personally enjoy and benefit from Shabbos, I could not imagine a more precious and enduring gift that any parent could give to his children.

As much as I was captivated by the idea of Shabbos, I was even more fascinated by another Jewish idea that has great potential to transform the social and spiritual landscape.

Purity of Speech

Ever since I was a child, I have felt uneasy around people who made fun of others, used foul language, swore in the name of God, or verbally harassed the vulnerable. Sometimes I was a victim and other times I was expected to approve of, if not collaborate in, such behaviour. Intuitively, I felt this was wrong, and often kept to myself. But derogatory speech was so ubiquitous, and the pressure to conform so relentless, that occasionally I wondered whether I was just oversensitive and there wasn't something, indeed, wrong with *me*.

---

26. In which case we are *obligated* to break the Shabbos, and not to do so would be in violation of the Torah.

There is an eye-opening parable that I heard during the Jerusalem Fellowship Program. A man, having spoken badly about his rabbi in public, felt remorse and went to him and apologized. Although the rabbi completely forgave him, the man inquired what he could do to make up for his misdemeanour. After some thought, the rabbi stated: "Go home, take your pillow outside and rip it open, exposing the feathers to the wind. Then come back and see me." The man, although perplexed by this directive, did exactly as the rabbi instructed. Upon returning shortly thereafter, the rabbi said: "Now, I want you to gather up all those feathers and bring them to me."

In this parable, the rabbi attempts to impress upon the man the seriousness of his "misdemeanour." Just as it is impossible to recover all the feathers that have been scattered by the wind, in the same manner, gossip, slander, slurs, and all forms of derogatory words, once released from the mouth, are spread quickly and irretrievably in all directions.

Purity of speech is a fundamental and powerful precept in Judaism. We may keep Shabbos every seven days, observe other holidays once a year, pray three times a day, visit the sick when the opportunity presents itself, give to charity regularly. But speaking? Some of us engage in this activity almost as often as thinking — and unfortunately, sometimes even more often! If there is one *mitzvah* (Biblical commandment) that has incredible potential for personal growth and self-transformation, it is the command to guard one's tongue.

There are many reasons why people initiate, listen to, or help spread derogatory information about others. They may have low self-esteem, and putting others down gives them a sense of superiority. Maybe they want to show off their wit. Perhaps they hope to accumulate friends — the juicy information in their possession guarantees them an audience. Or perhaps they seek to fill a lull in a conversation, or they simply find such activity fun.

Our sages teach that at least three parties are harmed by impure speech.

The victim is harmed in that her reputation, self-esteem, and perhaps business opportunities are at stake.

The listeners are harmed in that they are exposed to negative influences. Furthermore, their ability to relate to the victim as before has been irreparably compromised.

Finally, *the person engaging in impure speech* is harmed in that his level of spirituality is diminished. Demeaning others, whether the information is accurate or not, is self-demeaning. It also lowers one's social standing. The interest that other people may have in him is short-lived and tainted by mistrust. Just as he was capable of speaking badly about others to them, he will be capable of speaking badly about them to others when the opportunity arises.

The power of speech cannot be overestimated. One hurtful word, released inadvertently in the heat of the moment, can linger forever in the hearts of others, even if forgiven. Spoken at the opportune time, to the right audience, words can repair a relationship, or tear it apart. They can unite and inspire a community to action, or promote social divisiveness and incite people to violence. On a global level, words can trigger or prevent wars.

Impure speech does not pertain solely to *false* information about others. In instances when the information is true and accurate, one is forbidden from sharing it for no constructive purpose. Subtleties in facial expressions or tone of voice can also fall into the category of "impure speech," even though no actual words are spoken.

The laws of proper speech are not intuitive. Learning and practising the laws of proper speech is a lifelong process. The results are well worth the effort. Bitterness, jealousy, anger, and arrogance are purged from the hearts of those who habitually control their tongues. They become positive and influential role models in the complex realm of social or family interaction. Their souls shine through, revealing their godly selves rather than their earthly selves.

For the world, it fosters harmony and peace.

Pain and Suffering

From the moment Belinda and I began examining Judaism, one problem that crept into many discussions we had about God is this: How can a just and loving God have allowed the Holocaust to happen? Why do innocent people suffer? Why do bad things happen to good people? Is not pain proof that God does not exist?

Though it would be insensitive and inappropriate to offer intellectual arguments to address deep emotional hurts, there are a number of approaches to dealing with this issue for those of us whose denial of God may be purely intellectually driven. No one approach purports to explain satisfactorily any specific case of suffering, as humans are incapable of knowing the mind and calculations of God.

One of Judaism's most fundamental premises is that the greatest gift that God gives to humankind is free will: the ability to make moral choices and, in this manner, emulate God. If, each time a person acted wrongly, a quick bolt of electricity shocked him, and every time he did something moral, health and wealth greeted him, then very soon he (and others observing) would start to behave properly for immediate reward and would refrain from misdeeds to avoid punishment. In other words, the person would become an automaton in his decision-making and lose the ability to really choose and develop his morality. Delayed reward and punishment—even into the next life[27]—is one of many ways the Creator "hides His face" in order to maximize our free will and imbue our lives with meaning.

Pain or suffering is often a blessing in disguise. Consider Robert, a friend of Belinda's since college. One morning, he unexpectedly received a "pink slip" from his employer. Due to the company's restructuring, he was laid off along with some fifty other workers, and they were all ordered to leave the premises by noon of the same day. To his pleasant surprise, he landed a job with a competitor within days and received

---

27. The existence of an afterlife is a basic tenet of Judaism.

generous dismissal compensation from his ex-employer. On a more sombre level, many cancer survivors have stories of how their grave illness has totally changed their lives for the better.

I came to believe that "problems" are educationally necessary and inevitable. Each person has been put into this world for a unique purpose and must learn specific lessons to realize that purpose. Any lesson can be learned in countless ways, and exactly the same lesson can be learned through a small challenge as through a bigger one. "Be happy for the small problems in life," my sister once told me. Small problems seem to disappear when we have bigger problems to deal with.

In many cases, our afflictions and torments result from the actions of our fellow human beings: for example, acts of negligence that are rooted in apathy or self-absorption, or war triggered by greed or anger. Were God to intervene each time such things occurred, the responsibility that we have toward our fellow person would be severely compromised.

In the midst of suffering, attempting to rationalize God's existence may be very difficult. It is also an inappropriate diversion from the necessary task of dealing with one's loss or pain. Long-term hindsight makes it easier to see the guiding hand of God, though even then we may not always be able to do so.

Ultimately, God's calculations are infinitely too complex for any human being to grasp. This point cannot be overemphasized. Moreover, instead of asking, "How can God exist if I am suffering?" we can try, for a moment, to mentally detach ourselves from our painful circumstances and objectively ask a different question: Does not the experience of even a single moment of *pleasure* in my life call for awe and humility in judging my Creator — His creative power, His interest in me, not to mention His existence?

6

Growing Jewishly

*"If tomorrow you will be the same as you are today, what
for do you need tomorrow?"*

— author unknown

*I*t was a pleasant summer day. We had recently returned
from Israel and were relaxing in familiar surroundings.
Belinda showed me the cherry tree in her backyard. One
of the cherries was dark red and particularly inviting. She
plucked it, wiped it with her hands, and offered it to me. Not
accustomed to eating unwashed fruit, I graciously declined.
Belinda then — to my delighted surprise — thanked God for
the fruit, and put it in her mouth.

Perhaps the fact that the cherry came straight from the tree and not from a store made it easier to appreciate the hand of God in producing the fruit. In any case, something wonderful had just happened. I knew that Belinda's words were inspired by a genuine feeling of gratitude and were not intended to impress me. I wondered if from then on she would always recite blessings before eating different foods, and whether I would need to start doing the same. This single act at once elevated her spiritual status in my eyes and at the same time threatened my own lifestyle. Yet, at that moment, I loved my girlfriend more than I loved anyone else in the world.

A few weeks later, while we were running errands, Belinda mentioned that she wanted to buy a *siddur* (Jewish prayer book). All mundane preoccupations I had at that moment disappeared as a heightened sense of purpose took over. *A turning point*, I thought. As in the case of the cherry, I concealed the full extent of my emotions, not wanting her to associate her growth in Judaism with my happiness. Religious growth, I believed, needed to occur on its own terms.

I offered nonchalantly that, when time permitted, we could make a trip to a nearby Jewish bookstore that I heard had good prices. A few days later we dropped by this place. After Belinda purchased her siddur, I felt very proud of her. Not only was she spiritual, she was now spiritual in a *Jewish* context. After some consideration, I picked up a siddur for myself, as I did not own one. I felt uplifted.

It was a strange feeling, owning my own prayer book. I had always associated a siddur with lengthy and boring synagogue services, the only times I would ever use one. But, leafing through the pages of my new acquisition, it occurred to me that the siddur was intended to be used throughout an ordinary day — from the moment one wakes up in the morning until one falls asleep at night.

There are the blessings for the new day, blessings for different kinds of food, a blessing recited after relieving oneself in the bathroom. There is a special blessing upon witnessing lightning or thunder or seeing a rainbow, a blessing upon greeting a friend that one hasn't seen in a very long time, a blessing of gratitude upon surviving a life-threatening situation. There is a prayer for travelling; a prayer for bedtime; blessings and prayers for birth, marriage, death, and bereavement. How many times, I wondered, had I flipped through the pages of a siddur in synagogue and been oblivious to all of this? It's a typical example of realizing things when they become relevant, even though they may have been staring you in the face all along.

Prayer is not something reserved for the synagogue. According to Judaism, God is everywhere. God can be found as much in the home, as in the woods, and on the moon. God is — wherever we let Him in.

Before long, the siddur took on a fresh new character. As I started carrying it around and using it, it ceased to be "foreign" and was becoming a close and familiar companion.

One day, we found ourselves on an expressway that we rarely used. Rush hour was approaching, and cars were flying by.

With both hands gripping the wheel and eyes fixed on the road, I remarked to Belinda how inopportune our timing was and how dangerously fast some cars were zipping past us and changing lanes. Several minutes passed. Belinda asked me if I wanted a candy. The summer heat and stress of driving on that expressway had made my throat dry. "Sure," I replied, and partially opened my mouth. I expected her to slip the candy in, as she would normally do when both my hands were engaged in steering. This time was different. Belinda leaned toward me, put the candy halfway into my mouth and said, "Say a *berakhah* (blessing)." At first I thought she was joking. Then, when I realized she wasn't, I quickly debated how badly I needed the candy. Eventually, while trying not to get us killed, I concentrated and managed to recall most of the words of the blessing, after which she released the candy into my mouth. Here was someone very special, I thought. Perhaps a little crazy, but truly special.

※

And so, in the weeks and months following our return from Israel, Belinda and I gradually took on more and more observances. I began to wear a head covering and *tsitsis* (a special garment with ritual fringes). Although I had stopped using the telephone on Shabbos long before our trip, I continued to strengthen my level of Jewish observance, particularly with regard to Shabbos, the Jewish holidays, and the kosher dietary laws. In many other aspects, it was Belinda who led the way.

Confronting the Divinity of Torah

For the most part, the observances that Belinda and I undertook were infused with meaning and helped integrate and give concrete expression to our evolving worldview. They tended to be intellectually satisfying, psychologically fulfilling, and spiritually uplifting.

Nevertheless, we were faced with the challenge of committing to religious practices in cases when no tangible benefits were ascertainable. A prime example for me was abstaining from non-kosher food even when doing so would greatly inconvenience me, or praying at the prescribed hour of the day when no inspiration was present.

Perhaps imposing such rigid regulations and restrictions on a relatively relaxed lifestyle generated self-transforming humility: God — and no longer I — would occupy centre stage. The benefits would be immeasurable.

Becoming observant, however, seemed to require an onerous leap of faith. After all, what if a higher, intelligent being existed but did not author the Torah? Would we not be pitiable fools in falling for an extensive, demanding, and uncompromising bill of obligations, offered to us deceptively alongside glistening gems of timeless wisdom, which amounted to a tragic wasting of time?

I heard a beautiful analogy that helped me to come to terms with this question.

A doctor prescribes medication to his patients. A patient, unless he is medically savvy, will usually take the medication based on trust. Where does the trust come from? He may have been a patient of this doctor for years and been cured every time he got sick. He may have friends or relatives who reportedly had good experiences with this doctor. He may have heard through the media or word of mouth that this particular physician was reputable. Or perhaps he randomly pulls a name from the Yellow Pages, having acquired a fair degree of confidence in the medical establishment based on past experiences. In other words, *trust is based on information or evidence.*

Now, imagine that the patient has a serious illness, the doctor's prescription is highly potent, and the consequences of a mistake in the prescription would cost the patient his life. In this case, the patient's incentive to gather evidence about the reputability of the physician's medical knowledge and judgment is considerably greater. In other words, *the higher the stakes, the greater the incentive to seek evidence.*

Finally, it is not necessary (and, indeed, it is very rarely the case) to have one hundred percent proof that a doctor will not make a mistake before one decides to follow his or her orders, especially in cases when the implications of error are not serious. And, in such cases, if the potential consequences of *not* following the doctor's orders are serious enough, one will more likely follow the orders.

How does this analogy apply to our case? At a certain point during my investigation of religions, I realized that I could never be fully convinced of any particular religious system. Just as I could not be certain that Judaism represented the Truth, I could never be one hundred percent sure that it didn't. How, then, was I to live my life?

Well, how high were the stakes? What if the prescription for Jewish living, as expounded by Orthodox rabbis, was wrong? What were the worst consequences of endorsing the Torah way of life, and the worst consequences of not endorsing it? Judaism is a 3,300-year-old system that has proven itself, time and again, to be life affirming, psychologically healthy, grounded in wisdom, a system from which nobody ever died (except as a result of anti-Semitism). The more I learned about Judaism — its theology, its practices and traditions, and the positive effect it had in producing individuals, families, and communities with good, solid values — the more I wanted to be part of it.

This was not a blind leap of faith. It was trust. Trust is built on evidence and the prospect of more evidence with further investigation. A leap of faith, by contrast, occurs when one reaches a point in one's investigation where there simply are no more answers; one is called upon by the religious (or cult) authorities to "just believe" or "have faith."

☙

The more knowledgeable I became about the Jewish religion, the more I felt compelled to address the issue of my personal commitment to it. The matter was especially real to me as I wanted to start a family as soon as possible, and I needed to know whether the Torah was the word of God. If it was, and if Belinda eventually decided not to convert, then I was wasting precious time by dating her.

Ultimately, the rabbis' explanation of why a Jew is forbidden to marry a gentile — no matter how much the latter may be open to, and even following, a Jewish lifestyle — is, "God says so." The difference between a Jewish soul and a gentile soul is mystical.

While I continued to develop trust in the Torah and the rabbis through gathering evidence, the pressure to make a decision on the future of my relationship with Belinda was becoming unbearably great.

7

Trials and Tension

I was employed in the Municipality of Toronto Social Services Department for almost five years, assessing applicants' eligibility for welfare assistance, and I had become increasingly bored. Over the previous year or two I looked for more challenging employment, a job with greater opportunity for upward mobility. More recently, the municipality was seeking to lay off staff and was offering generous voluntary severance packages. In November 1996, I received a phone call regarding an intriguing position with the Correctional Service of Canada, for which I had applied two years previously. I attended the interview, and was accepted the same day. My first assignment would be to work in a maximum-security penitentiary in Kingston starting in early January. Kingston is a small city, about a three-hour drive from Toronto.

Immediately I investigated the city's Jewish infrastructure. It had only one Orthodox synagogue, for which they were still seeking a rabbi after the previous one had left months earlier. There was not a single restaurant, store, or bakery that was kosher. I was told there were only about one or two thousand Jews in Kingston.

The city itself, as I was to discover later, is quite pretty. Situated alongside Lake Ontario, it boasts many historical attractions, colourful cafés and patios, live theatre, and numerous cultural festivals and events. Outdoor recreational opportunities abound, including hiking, bird watching, sailing, and fishing. With a population of less than 120,000, Kingston had all the conveniences of big city Toronto, while being spared the noise, traffic, long-distance commuting, pollution, and outrageous real-estate costs. It was a healthy and affordable place to live.

Hopeful Separation

I discussed the job prospect with Belinda at length. She needed to stay in Toronto because of her job and the necessity to help support her family. The question was whether I should go, and leave her behind.

The decision was very difficult. I knew that after a year or two of working in the prison, there would be an opportunity to transfer to Toronto and work in the parole area. I also thought that the separation might give each of us some needed space, which could be healthy for our relationship. At that stage, we were still "sticky rice" (though no longer in public), and the reduced opportunities for physical contact would be in line with Rabbi Pomerantz's advice that I had received five months earlier.

On the down side, I would be leaving the vibrant Toronto Jewish community that had nourished me immeasurably since I met Belinda, a community to which I had become increasingly attached and where most of my friends were.

Even more important was the emotional difficulty of being separated from my girlfriend. It had been more than two years since we met. Belinda was everything I sought in a soul mate. Her devotion to her family impressed me. For years she worked diligently to save money and then purchased a house to accommodate them when they immigrated. Her generosity also extended to total strangers. Thank-you letters and receipts appeared constantly in her mailbox from a plethora of charitable organizations, some of which I had never even heard of. Among other causes, Belinda sent money to the Foster Parents Plan. She corresponded with a couple of foster children in different African villages, underprivileged kids she had never met and yet whose lives she helped improve. I once asked her if she knew where in Africa those countries were located. She had no idea. It didn't matter.

Belinda was fully comfortable with her heritage. Unlike many immigrants who are eager to dive into the melting pot once they set foot in North America, Belinda, if we were blessed with children, would raise them in her native tongue, even though she was fluent in English. Also, she would be fully supportive of my speaking Yiddish. This might sound trite, yet, no Jewish women I had ever dated had had an affirmative attitude toward this maltreated Jewish language. That meant a lot to me.

That Belinda was not one to follow the crowd became apparent the day she introduced me to Kornie—her minuscule corn snake, now more than four feet long. Although I lacked any affinity for reptiles and wondered why anyone, especially a bright, affable, young woman, would choose to own a cold-blooded, self-seeking pet that seemed to spend its life hiding in dark places, I was drawn to Belinda's unabashed individualism and her fondness for living creatures.

We finally decided that I should accept the job offer. We figured that we could visit each other on weekends and maintain contact by telephone, e-mail, or letters. We made a house-hunting trip together and succeeded in locating an apartment within walking distance (albeit forty minutes) of the synagogue, so that I would be able to attend services on Shabbos.

The evening before I departed for Kingston, we went for a long walk around the Holiday Inn in Toronto, where I had been staying for the previous few days after vacating my apartment. It was January 4. A new year had begun. Christmas lights were everywhere. Although they had no religious significance for Belinda or me, the lights created a special atmosphere that could not be ignored. I felt lonely and excited and apprehensive and hopeful all at the same time. Melancholic contemplation on being separated from

Belinda, happy thoughts of beginning a new career, excitement and fear of working with dangerous offenders, and anticipation of getting to know a new city and discovering a small, remote Jewish community — all competed for attention. Most of all, I felt that Belinda and I were at a turning point in our relationship, for better or worse, and deep down I was confident about the decision we had made.

I slowed my gait and looked at Belinda. "I'd like to marry you," I said.

She stared at me. "Pardon me?"

"I said...I'd like to marry you. But the only thing that prevents me from proposing is that the Torah prohibits intermarriage."

"I see." We continued walking.

"I could go against the will of my parents, of all my relatives, my friends, and even the entire Jewish community, but I can't go against the will of our Creator," I added, feeling a need to justify my previous remark.

"Well..." Belinda stopped abruptly and turned to me, a faint smile emerging. "I'm happy that the Torah prohibition bothers you — because it bothers me too. I, too, feel it would be wrong to intermarry."

I breathed easier. At least, we were on the same wavelength.

Criminal Encounters

Working with offenders enabled me to appreciate Judaism significantly more than I would have otherwise. I learned firsthand that although there are all kinds of crimes, and offenders come in all shapes and sizes, there are common predictors of criminality. These include coming from broken families, drug and alcohol addictions, unstable employment history, volatile relationships, and poor literacy and interpersonal skills. Such conditions also exist in society as a whole, though to a lesser degree, and even less within Orthodox Jewish circles.

Having a sense of purpose and direction in life usually enables the self-discipline that is crucial for an offender to address his or her needs effectively. Institutional programming or the prospect of an early release is insufficient. The offenders who succeed in permanently changing their lifestyle are those who are internally motivated to do so.

Despite inmates' greater needs, stronger temptations, and higher vulnerabilities, the standards of acceptable conduct for inmates are not set any higher than those that exist in the rest of society. Derogatory language, as long as it is not intimidating, is tolerated. Idleness, because it is not outlawed in the broader society, cannot be condemned. Nor, except in special circumstances, can staff censure the kinds of books or television programs to which inmates often expose themselves. Being protected by the Canadian Constitution, inmates are entitled to all the rights that every Canadian citizen enjoys (including the right to vote in federal elections), with few exceptions. These are the rights, notably mobility, that need to be curtailed for the safety of the public or of the correctional institution.

The stark implication of this liberal, minimal-interventionist philosophy was brought home to me through the following *graphic* account.

One of my first clients was a middle-aged man whose girlfriend had caught him raping her six-year-old daughter at their home. Upon being discovered, he killed his girlfriend as well as the daughter and proceeded to have sexual intercourse with the dead bodies. He then cut them up and set fire to the house.

That evening I arrived home depressed. Seeking instant distraction, I turned on the television and flipped through the channels. I came across a movie scene in which a man was tied up and repeatedly tortured. Sitting in the comfort of my living room and viewing this (only for a few minutes before turning off the television in disgust), I couldn't help wondering if my fellow Canadian citizen was watching the same program in his cell.

For the most part, offenders make little distinction between morality and legality. Once I interviewed a seasoned "career criminal," a chronic hold-up robber and property thief, who had applied for early release. I asked him what would make me think he wouldn't return to his criminal ways. He had been in and out of prisons more than a dozen times in the previous twenty years.

"Because of the consequences," he stated matter-of-factly, referring to incarceration.

"What if you are not caught?" I challenged him.

"Because of the consequences," he repeated himself.

"No, no. Imagine for a moment that it is *one hundred percent certain* that you will not be caught. Why would you not do it again?"

Again, he replied "because of the consequences."

This went on a couple more times. Then, sensing that I was running thin on patience, he thought for a moment and added: "If I knew for sure that I would not be caught, then I would do it again. And then again. And yet again. And so on, until eventually I *would* be caught! So—because of the consequences," he stated with finality.

This was an example, perhaps somewhat extreme, of a person who had no sense at all that his actions were harmful to society, or if he did, he did not care. He thought solely of himself and the possible consequences to *him*.

Where does such a mindset come from? Whereas moral law operates on the assumption that actions and behaviours are intrinsically good or bad regardless of whether there are obvious consequences attached, the criminal justice system operates on more bureaucratic principles. Thus, an offender is someone who has been caught and convicted of breaching a legal code. He is not "bad" but "legally challenged." He does not have to answer to God or to society, but only to the criminal justice system. "Doing time" wipes the slate clean. Remorse is not a mandatory requirement to be granted eventual release.

Legality has all but replaced morality in the cold, hard criminal world. And because the laws of the land are human-made and constantly being amended, how can anyone, least of all offenders, be expected to obey them?

❦

Most weekends I stayed in Kingston, where the new rabbi and his wife, or other observant families, would often invite me for a Shabbos meal. There were a handful of observant families in Kingston.

About once a month I would leave work early on Friday afternoon to make the three-hour trip to Toronto and arrive barely in time for Shabbos. Belinda would have arranged for our hosts, accepting offers from friends or acquaintances, or sometimes just calling up some religious families and inviting ourselves. (The going joke in the community was that I was being let out of prison on a weekend pass.) It was not uncommon to sleep over at others' homes when the walk to Belinda's house was far.

In the process of making Shabbos arrangements on a regular basis for herself and her "Shabbos buddy," Lucy, and about once a month for me as well, Belinda strengthened and expanded her network of friends and acquaintances within the Orthodox community.

Whether in Kingston or Toronto, Shabbos was an oasis of sanity. The warmth and glow of Shabbos, the safety of being among fellow God-centric people (even if we had never met before), and the heightened moral consciousness that an observant Jewish lifestyle inspired, contrasted starkly with the cold, dangerous, and depressing work environment from which I would regularly take refuge and to which I would all too soon need to return.

A Feeling of Imprisonment

Belinda and I were compatible in infinite ways. Thanks to our relationship, I was able to discover authentic Judaism. This was in part because my deep desire to please my parents and relatives, coupled with my own thinking about the moral education of our prospective children, forced me to think very seriously about religion. I felt a tremendous debt of gratitude to the Creator for having brought the two of us together.

Belinda and I inspired each other toward Jewish religious growth, including real change in how we looked at the world. We were now at the point — after two and a half years of looking into Judaism as well as other religions — where we believed that the Torah was from God and that, therefore, a Jew must marry only a Jew.

As of March 1997, Belinda had been considering conversion for well over a year. However, she consistently expressed to me that she hated the idea that our relationship should be contingent on her becoming Jewish. She felt strongly that a person's decision to become Jewish was a very personal one, between oneself and God, and that one should not convert for the sake of keeping a relationship, no matter how wonderful the relationship may be. She told me many times that three things held her back from making a decision to become Jewish: she wanted to be one hundred percent sure that it was not because of my influence; she wanted to be one hundred percent sure that she would be capable of fulfilling all the applicable mitzvos (she was somewhat of a perfectionist); and, finally, she recognized that becoming Jewish required accepting the validity of the Torah in its entirety[28] and every once in a while she came across a concept that did not "sit right" with her.

Hardly a day would pass that I did not ask myself — and God — numerous times whether I should end the relationship. We no longer had physical contact, but we were still committed to dating each other exclusively. If the Torah prohibited intermarriage, then, logically, interdating must be wrong as well, because the purpose of dating is marriage.

Belinda's biological clock was ticking, and somehow it was ticking even louder in my consciousness than hers. I constantly wondered how much longer I should wait for her to decide whether she wanted to become Jewish. It was true that all the signs and indicators pointed toward eventual conversion — and

28. Questioning or debating with the goal of learning is encouraged and expected for gentiles seriously considering Orthodox conversion. Rejecting the divine nature of the Torah is not, for it does not reflect whole-hearted commitment to its laws and precepts.

that is precisely why I felt it might be wrong to break off the relationship. It would have been a much easier decision for me had Belinda shown signs of becoming less and less interested in Judaism.

I felt I was locked inside a spiritual prison, and no one but God had the keys to let me out. I didn't know how long it would take for Belinda to make a decision, and she didn't know either. I was consistently opposed to putting pressure on her, both on practical and philosophical grounds. Waiting passively for an indefinite time affected my physical health, manifesting itself in an array of digestive disorders. Breaking up might not only be emotionally devastating for her, it might not help her make an honest decision about conversion, because, in the back of her mind, she would know that if she later converted, she could probably get back together with me.

Kingston was lonely in the evenings. Sometimes, when the air was warm and the day long, I would take a walk by myself along the water. I would fantasize that I was back at Algonquin Park. The scene would always be the same.

> I am sitting comfortably on the cool ground, kindling a fire. Behind me is a wide, still lake. The air is warm, the sun is setting, and there are no mosquitoes. I look up and see Belinda walking, leisurely, in my direction, carrying some food. She is sporting a light brown nylon jacket, a yellow baseball cap, a knee-length blue-jean skirt, and white running shoes. Except for the skirt, she looks exactly as she did in previous times when we went camping.

I greet her with a smile. She reciprocates and sits beside me, facing me at an angle. We eat. We sit for a very long time. We do not exchange a word. I am happy to enjoy our surroundings with her. There is no need to talk. There is nothing to say. After all, she is now Jewish. *Jewish!* There is no tension, no hidden agenda. I am at peace.

Belinda told me in March that since my move to Kingston two months earlier, she had been able to see more clearly that she liked to attend Jewish events for herself, without my company. One day, in a phone conversation, she raised the matter of her ambivalence with regard to conversion.

I seized the opportunity and suggested that, were I in her shoes, I would start the conversion process, knowing that I could always change my mind at any time. Following the advice of my brother in Philadelphia, I said to her that the only way to know if one really liked water and swimming, was to jump into the pool. Otherwise, I added, one could become paralyzed by uncertainty.

What did becoming Jewish entail? As I anxiously researched the matter, I was awed and dismayed by how weighty the process was. I did not share with Belinda what I learned: an Orthodox conversion generally requires at least one complete year of formal study — often much longer — which gives the candidate the opportunity to build her knowledge base and experience all the Jewish holidays at least once. Moreover, it gives the *Beis Din* (rabbinical court) the ability to carefully assess the candidate's sincerity and his or her potential to integrate into a religious community. Above all, becoming Jewish according to the Orthodox stream of Judaism requires a sincere and total commitment to following all the Torah laws.

Once the Beis Din is convinced of the candidate's sincerity and satisfied with her level of knowledge, observance, and commitment, the ceremony takes place. Becoming Jewish is considered a rebirth. A Hebrew name is chosen, and the candidate must completely immerse herself in a ritual body of water called a *mikvah*.[29] If the candidate is male, a circumcision is performed as well.

I looked up the Conservative, Reform, and Reconstructionist guidelines for conversion, and compared them with those of the Orthodox denomination. Surprisingly, although the former were more lenient, they were fairly demanding as well. All denominations regarded conversion as a very serious matter. I wondered if an alternative to an Orthodox conversion might be good enough for the time being. "Accepting Judaism to the exclusion of all other religious faiths and practices...promising to establish a Jewish home and to participate actively in the life of the synagogue and of the Jewish community...promising to rear one's children as Jews...committing oneself to the pursuit of Torah and Jewish knowledge...pledging loyalty to Judaism and to the Jewish people under all circumstances"—all this, which has been endorsed by the Reform movement,[30] seemed meaningful.

29. From whence arose the Christian practice of baptism.
30. Epstein, Lawrence. *Conversion to Judaism:* A Guidebook (Northvale, New Jersey, Jason Aronson Inc., 1994).

However, converting outside the Orthodox framework, I knew, was wishful thinking. Belinda and I came to respect the teachings of Orthodox Judaism and we were well aware that Orthodox Judaism did not recognize any of the other denominations as valid expressions of the faith (a fact that both saddened and intrigued me). Were she to convert through the Conservative or Reform movement and we were to marry, it would be considered an intermarriage from the Orthodox perspective, something I could not live with.

I did not know whether Belinda had started looking into the process of conversion. The issue was very sensitive, so I was afraid to even ask her as I did not want her to feel the least bit pressured. She wanted so much to know that any decision to convert would be her very own personal one. I respected and admired this genuineness, and told her so numerous times. The problem was that I did not know what I should do for myself.

✤

At the end of March, I spent Shabbos in Toronto. Belinda and I talked for five hours. She told me that she had started the conversion process and had not informed me earlier because she did not want to raise my hopes in the event that she were to change her mind. Another reason was that she was not one hundred percent sure that she wanted to convert, and she did not want to risk the possibility that I might influence her. She further said that she would like to avoid "reporting" to me on her progress or lack thereof, and she requested that I not get involved.

Belinda told me that she had started responding to my mother's letter. This was a letter my mother had written to Belinda almost a year earlier, emphasizing how difficult it is to be Jewish and urging her to end the relationship with me, to which Belinda could not bring herself to reply.

Over the next few weeks, she completed her reply and gave it to me to translate into Italian and send to my mother.

Letter to my mother, dated March 21, 1997:

Dear Mrs. Botwinik,

Thank you for writing to my family and me in May 1996. Please accept this letter as my belated response to you, and my apology for not communicating to you until now.

I am happy for Yankl to have caring parents such as you and Mr. Botwinik. I understand the relationship between Yankl and me is a sensitive matter to your family. Your concern regarding our having different religions is legitimate, and I appreciate your openness in letting me know how you feel.

Mrs. Botwinik, I was not raised with any particular religion and I never believed in God. The relationship between Yankl and me introduced me to Judaism, which has helped me to develop the awareness of God and grow tremendously as a person. The relationship has also helped Yankl discover the Truth in his religion. Both of us feel that we have grown and benefited significantly from the relationship, which we hold very dearly.

I like the teachings of Judaism, and I believe it holds more truth than any other religion that I have investigated. I agree with you that it is difficult to be Jewish. I am presently examining the possibility of conversion, for I do like the positive influence Judaism has on me, and its potential to do the same for my children. I strongly dislike the intention to convert for the sole benefit of the relationship. I believe it would only lead to failure in the long run. I am sorry that I am unable to offer you an answer that could address your concerns, at the present time.

I wish to grow and learn with Yankl, and continue to explore Judaism for its own sake. I hope this letter can offer you a better understanding of me, and my perspective on the issue. Yankl and I both want to build a family as soon as appropriate, and we often discuss this matter, which may greatly affect our future together. Mrs. Botwinik, I am sorry if it has made you feel that my exploration of Judaism is holding up one of your children's lives. I can imagine it must be very difficult for any caring parent to be in a situation that you and Mr. Botwinik are in. Yankl and I understand that time is precious, but a hasty decision may cost even more time in the long run.

I will be happy to hear from you again and share my thoughts with you for any other concerns that you may have regarding Yankl's and my relationship. I feel that I have obtained more clarity of our situation, and I am confident that I will be able to respond to you in a more timely fashion. I hope to communicate to you in writing through Yankl.

Yours truly,

Belinda

One day Belinda posed the following question to me: Suppose you found out that you were not Jewish, would you convert? I thought about it all through my three-hour drive back to Kingston. I called Belinda a few days later and told her that, given how much I knew about Judaism, I *believed* and *hoped* that I would convert, but acknowledged that I did not honestly know if I would go ahead with it. Belinda responded, "This is exactly the situation I am facing."

In the middle of April, Belinda and I flew to Philadelphia to spend Passover with my brother and his in-laws. They are affiliated with Conservative Judaism and invited us to join them. During our visit, I took a long walk with Belinda. She told me that she felt a little distant from me. I replied that this was to be expected as long as she chose to keep me ignorant of her personal journey with Judaism and the conversion process. Belinda asked what she could do in order to involve me in her process while at the same time not allowing my influence to affect her. I was at a loss for suggestions.

We decided that upon our return to Toronto we would seek advice from a rabbi we liked and respected, and whom we knew had considerable experience counselling young people involved in interdating.

We met with Rabbi Sobalman on a Sunday morning. Stepping into his modest house, surrounded by exotic works of fine art, including several colourful three-dimensional creations protruding from the walls, I quickly dispelled any persistent image of Orthodox rabbis as a bland, homogeneous group.

The rabbi listened attentively to our story. Because he was Orthodox, we were half expecting him to advise us to break off the relationship until and unless Belinda decided for sure that she wanted to become Jewish. This did not happen. The rabbi concluded that the situation was "very complex;" it was obvious from what we were telling him that Belinda was seriously pursuing Judaism and trying to get at the Truth. He suggested she write down the questions that were troubling her (for example, the practice of animal sacrifices during the time of the Holy Temple) and seek answers. He also suggested that we consider negotiating a time limit — a certain number of months — after which we would have to make a decision whether or not to separate.

We chose not to set a time limit, agreeing it would be too stressful.

Later that month, Belinda informed her family that she was considering Judaism as her religion. They were supportive. When Belinda was a child, her mother had always told her that any religion that she might choose for herself would be fine with her. In fact, two of Belinda's siblings became Protestant Christians.

At this point, Belinda still faced the same impediments in deciding to become Jewish. Time and again I took it upon myself to address them. We would have long and deep conversations in the cool basement of her house, slouched on an old sofa, blankets tossed over us, and quiet music in the background. Belinda's mother and siblings would typically be upstairs, going about their business, oblivious to the spiritual challenges that preoccupied us.

"Judaism does not demand perfection — only a sincere commitment to try one's best," I lectured. "And there is no reason to assume that a convert who occasionally slipped in her level of observance would be judged more harshly than a returnee to Judaism — for example, myself — who did the same."

In general, Belinda very much liked listening to me talk. It was one of the things that attracted her to me. She also felt I was exceptionally polite.

"Regarding the necessity to believe that the entire Torah is true," I continued, "learning Judaism is a lifelong process, and there will always be issues that we will not understand or that will bother us. So, establishing absolute veracity is not a realistic goal. However, we can look at Judaism as a whole and ask ourselves whether it represents a system for personal growth and fulfillment, as well as *tikkun olam* (fixing or improving the world), that is unequalled."

"I'm not sure I agree," Belinda returned, unenthused. "In any case, the most challenging matter for us is the possible influence from the relationship. If we were to break up, the influence would still be there because the possibility to get back together would speak to my subconscious. So either way, it would be impossible for me to decide whether or not to convert outside the influence of the relationship — unless you died, God forbid, or discovered that you were a *Kohen*."[31]

"Bel, there is nothing wrong with influence *per se* — in fact, we all have a responsibility to influence one another positively." I tried to contain my frustration, while mustering every ounce of oratory skills I had. "All that matters is whether the influence is positive or negative. In other words, do you really like Judaism, or were you brainwashed by me to *think* you like it? Furthermore, I don't think that there is anything wrong with converting in order to render a marriage permissible by Jewish law, as long as that is not the *primary* motive for wanting to convert. After all, Judaism is not just a private relationship between the individual and the Creator, it is also about family and community, and if you and I are compatible for building a strong Jewish family, there is nothing wrong for that to be a strong motivating factor for conversion."

"I know for sure that I like Judaism very much; I just don't know if I like it *enough* that I would want to convert if you were not in the picture, especially considering how demanding Judaism is. I could simply be a Noahide."

31. A member of the priestly class of Jews who have certain unique ritual responsibilities and are prohibited from marrying converts.

And so we explored and analyzed and debated over and over. One day I had an insight: "Listen, if the decision to become Jewish must be entirely personal, as you insist, then the decision for you to *not* become Jewish also has to be entirely personal. Let me ask you this: Suppose your entire family and all your relatives suddenly became fascinated with Judaism, and soon after converted — would you let that influence your own decision whether or not to convert?"

I think that gave her some (kosher) food for thought!

8

Resolution

I spent Shabbos in Toronto. Belinda told me that she would *probably* become Jewish. She reasoned that if, for whatever reason, our relationship were to end, she would not want to marry someone who believed in Jesus, nor an atheist, but someone who believed in one God and in the Torah. Two options remained: to date other Noahides or date a Jew. The latter option would recreate the same situation as present. As for dating Noahides, the problem was that there were so very few of them. Moreover, they had no substantial community of their own as do people of other religions. The closest community available to them was the religious Jewish community. Thus Belinda drew the conclusion that in her current growth-oriented situation, to remain a Noahide would be more difficult than converting and living as a Jew.

Although I welcomed this turn of events, it did not satisfy my longing for certitude. "Probably become Jewish" did not point to a time frame for marriage.

In the course of the next few weeks, I crafted a letter indicating my intention to end the relationship. It had been almost one year since the trip to Israel and my meeting with Rabbi Pomerantz, who had suggested a one-year deadline. Despite the hopeful indicators, there was no definitive statement from Belinda that she would become Jewish. My patience had all but run its course.

Here is the full text of this letter:

Dear Bel,

It's very difficult for me to write this. I want to tell you that I think it is better at this point in our relationship that we separate.

You know of my strong desire to get married and establish a warm Jewish home as soon as possible. It is something that occupies my mind numerous times during the days (fortunately, I'm still able to sleep!).

Perhaps more than ever before, I consider us to be very compatible as life partners. My love for you is as strong as ever. However, we seem to be "stuck." It is an unhealthy experience, as far as I am concerned. As long as the issue of intermarriage bothers us, the issue of interdating should also bother us, since the purpose of dating is marriage.

It is possible that one day I (or you, or both of us) will come to the conclusion that HaShem[32] does not really "care" about intermarriage, that the references in the Torah are not true and we have been fooling ourselves all this time to believe otherwise. Then, our break-up would, tragically, have been in vain.

Be that as it may, we have to proceed *now* by what we now believe to be the case — i.e., that the Torah is true. As long as this is our view, we should not be dating. Simply put, that would be the mature thing to do.

Over time, we have gotten more distant from each other physically and, lately, geographically. Spiritually and emotionally, I feel I have actually gotten closer to you. The problem is, I am looking for someone to *marry* — not merely a friendship relationship, no matter how special.

Several things have been happening around my family that I avoided telling you because I did not want you to feel pressured to become Jewish or to break up with me. For example, numerous letters have been flying around between Montreal, Israel, Kingston, and Philadelphia concerning our

32. Literally, it means "the Name." It refers to God.

situation; expensive telephone bills, health-related problems on the part of my parents from anguish/worry. (Of course, I did not keep you totally in the dark—because that would not be fair either.) I felt that with my other friends (e.g., Richard in Montreal, Helen, Frank, et cetera) I could discuss these problems that I have been experiencing more freely than with my own girlfriend. (Of course, this was my own choice and no fault of yours.) This is not a very healthy way to live.

The point is that my family is very important to me, as I know yours is to you…I especially miss my mother.

I am not telling you this because I want to say that my family comes before my relationship with you. I was always aware of the mitzvah to honour one's father and mother, but I also felt that I was not doing anything wrong by dating you. Now I am not sure whether dating you is okay, but I *am* still sure that honouring one's parents is right. As long as the two activities are incompatible, I can choose only one. I have to go by the one that I know for sure is right. Does this make sense?

Still, the main reason I think we should separate is that the longer we "date" each other—if in the end it doesn't work out between us—the harder it will be to separate and find a husband/wife.

If I can't have the first choice (because HaShem wills it to be so) I need to look for the "second best."

I have never believed that you should become Jewish for the sake of the relationship. In fact, if I were to find out tomorrow that I was not Jewish, then, given our present strong interest in Judaism, we would probably also have to separate—because if only one of us eventually decided to become Jewish and not the other, it would constitute "intermarriage"! We would both have to make a decision one way or the other, before determining whether we should resume dating.

I never imagined that I would be dating someone for three years without marrying her. I always thought in terms of a few months. Of course, in retrospect, it was necessary for us to date for so long, given our very different cultural backgrounds. Recently (around November or December) I came to the conclusion that you and I would likely share the same vision of how we would build our lives and home together. At that point, I felt a very strong urge to propose marriage to you, for I do not believe in unnecessary waiting. Something held me back, and I am pretty sure it was the "technicality" in the Book of Deuteronomy...

Thanks to our relationship, we have both grown a lot, and I see the world in a very different (more mature) way than before I met you. You told me you do as well. I am very glad. It seems that our relationship was meant to be, at least up until a point.

If you still have a desire to tackle the challenges of our relationship, and make it work, I am very supportive. Recently you have indicated many times that the relationship itself (i.e., "my influence"), and not the prohibition against intermarriage (with which you seem to be in agreement), may be the greatest obstacle. That being the case, the most logical solution is for us to separate. From my point of view, dating serves the primary purpose of getting to know one another to test marriage compatibility. Although one can never be one hundred percent sure of anything, I reached the point where I feel that I know you well enough to want to marry you.

I never sent the letter. I told myself that twelve months had indeed passed, but that I would tack on an additional month because of how close she was to deciding to convert. As it turned out, shortly before the thirteenth month was over, Belinda told me that she would be scheduling a meeting with the Beis Din.

Shortly thereafter, I sent a note of this news to my parents. My mother called back, and I spoke to my father for the first time since Rosh HaShanah of the previous year. At his request, Belinda and I arranged a brief meeting in Kingston, where Belinda told them in person that she intended to become Jewish.

From that day on, I began to communicate once again with my father.

Court Appearance

I was very excited and looking forward to meeting with the Beis Din. I envisioned myself impressing them with my fluent Yiddish and extensive cultural Jewish background (trips to Israel, summers on a kibbutz, eleven years of Jewish education), as well as my recent growth in Torah knowledge and observance. Most of all, I was very eager to see the prospect of Belinda converting—and the prospect of our eventual marriage—becoming more real.

On November 19, 1997, I took the day off and drove to Toronto for our first scheduled meeting with the Beis Din. Belinda had met with them once before by herself. They were situated in a large building that served primarily as an educational and administrative centre for *Lubavitch.*[33]

Three elderly, bearded rabbis in white shirts and dark suits sat behind a table, facing Belinda and me. The secretary of the Beis Din, himself a rabbi of a congregation, was also present. After quick, cursory introductions, one of them began to speak. He said that the résumé Belinda had prepared was impressive, and he immediately began to pose pointed questions to her about the Jewish religion. Belinda responded well, and I felt

---

33. A dynamic, worldwide Hassidic group that engages extensively in outreach. One member of the rabbinical court was a Lubavitcher. The others were not.

proud of her. I myself did not know the answers to some of the questions. After some ten minutes, they suddenly turned to me and wanted to know my level of observance. I was interrogated: Do you put on *tefillin* every day? Do you have a mezuzah at every doorpost? Do you shave with a blade?[34] Do you observe the Shabbos?

They were not pleased with my replies. They told me, half jokingly, that Belinda was more "advanced" than I, and that if I didn't become completely observant they would have to find her another boyfriend!

I spoke to them in Yiddish. I also spoke Hebrew and English. I informed them that my father had grown up in a religious home and left when he was about nineteen to escape the war; he never saw his family again. I had an observant brother and sister in Israel. I told them that my goal was to become entirely *frum* (observant), and that I was slowly progressing toward this goal. They responded that when I met with them next time, they would like to hear from me that I was putting on tefillin every day, and that I no longer shaved using a blade. The meeting lasted twenty minutes.

At the end, I started asking a question, but they quickly excused themselves, explaining that they were in a hurry to leave for another appointment. The secretary apologized and

34. According to Orthodox Judaism, a Jew is not permitted to shave with a blade. An electric razor is permitted, since it applies a scissor-like action to cut the beard hairs.

explained that he too needed to leave right away. He left me his telephone number and e-mail address.

Upon my return to Kingston, I e-mailed the secretary my burning question: How close was Belinda to being approved for conversion? His prompt and cordial response was that the conversion was only going to happen when *I*, "and not just Belinda," was fully and one hundred percent committed to Judaism. Any compromises in my or her observance would not do.

I felt the muscles in my body go limp. I stared at the words for a long time: "fully and one hundred percent committed." I thought this might be an impossible goal to achieve. How could I commit myself totally to a system that I still understood only at a relatively superficial level, and about which I had more questions than answers? And if eventually it was going to happen, who knows how many years it could take?

The tables were turned. This must be exactly what Belinda had been struggling with all these months.

For the first time, I felt that I needed to start worrying more about my own observance of the Torah and less about my girlfriend's. She might quickly surpass me, if she hadn't done so already. And once that happened, I would have to face the real possibility that she would be impeded in her conversion because of my own lack of growth and total commitment.

Even presenting herself before the Beis Din with a Jew who didn't put on tefillin reflected poorly on her.

With consternation, it became patently clear to me that the Beis Din would not consider speeding up the process of conversion because of my wanting to marry Belinda, because of our ages and desire to have a large family, nor for any other reason. They were very suspicious of romantic motives. For them, one thing mattered: Belinda must convince each member of the Beis Din that she was entirely dedicated to a religious lifestyle, and (in the firm and unyielding words of the secretary) "would do whatever the Torah demanded, whether she liked it or not." The entire initiative and responsibility must come from her. Conversion is for eternity, because even after death, the soul remains Jewish.

The Beis Din was informed that Belinda practised ritual hand-washing every morning, recited the morning and evening blessings, recited blessings before and after eating, and upon exiting the washroom. The rabbis knew that she went to classes twice per week (in addition to her conversion classes), followed the laws of modest dress, gave to charity, endeavoured to observe the laws of proper speech, bought kosher foods for herself, kindled Shabbos candles, and attended synagogue and Jewish events. All this did not seem to be enough.

Belinda's process of switching to keeping kosher was very gradual and took more than a year. She had started by insisting that all junk food she ate be kosher. After discovering that many kinds of chocolate, chips, and ice cream that she liked were in fact kosher, she figured that the struggle of not eating the non-kosher ones should be manageable. Some months later she eliminated non-kosher animals from her diet. Her mother would use chicken or beef instead of pork when cooking for the family. Soon vegetarian oyster sauce replaced regular oyster sauce, and other restrictions were introduced. Belinda told me that when she wasn't home for a meal, her mother sometimes took full advantage and cooked all pork dishes for the rest of the family!

The final step was the hardest. Belinda set up a very basic kosher kitchen for herself in the basement (her sister kindly gave up some of her study space for this purpose) and began purchasing groceries and cooking for herself. She tried to time her cooking so that she could eat with everyone else, albeit from her own separate plates. Above and beyond the physical inconveniences, her mother's cooking was by far her favourite, and to no longer partake of it while seated at the same table was emotionally very difficult for both of them. Although Belinda's mother did not understand the changes in her daughter's lifestyle, she was very respectful. She even began learning the kosher symbols and looked for kosher ingredients for her daughter when she shopped.

Belinda's family saw and lived through the changes with her. She had chosen a way of life that has been practised for the past 3,300 years, and yet was extremely foreign to them. Despite all the seemingly strange things that she did, especially on Shabbos, they were very supportive. For this, Belinda was deeply grateful. Her siblings bought her, for her birthday and other occasions, a kosher cookbook, a CD to help her learn Hebrew, and a beautifully framed text of the "Shema" blessing, which proclaims the oneness of God. On Friday nights, her siblings would set the lights in the house and turn them off at the appropriate time, even though she did not ask them to do so.

At this point, Belinda had some four months of formal conversion classes left. A woman recommended by the Beis Din who specialized in teaching female conversion candidates gave these classes one on one. Belinda thought that the Beis Din would want her to live in an environment that would best foster her Jewish growth, one wherein it would be easier to keep kosher, Shabbos, and other Jewish observances. As such, she suspected that the Beis Din would require her to live apart from her family as a condition for her conversion. (This turned out not to be the case.)

Belinda continued with her conversion classes as I waited impatiently. I began to push myself to make more progress in my own observance, in anticipation of future encounters with the Beis Din. These encounters were frequently cancelled or postponed for a variety of reasons, adding to my frustration.

The months were passing. Soon I started questioning my own motives for becoming observant. True, I had no doubt that a lot of things that I now did were a result of my changing worldview, insight, and appreciation of Judaism. But it was quite possible that I would have progressed more slowly were it not for the fact that Belinda's conversion hinged on my own observance level. As it was, I began to ask myself: Am I putting on tefillin every day (as opposed to, say, once a week) because of Belinda and the prospect of marriage, or am I doing it solely for myself? I knew that the answer was, in part, the former. This, I later realized, did not represent true growth; and even after Belinda's conversion, it took a long time until I felt that I really "owned" some of my commitments.

Belinda was right: if one converts to Judaism for the sake of marriage, then there is no intrinsic motivation to maintain the attained level of observance after the wedding.

Armed for Life

Belinda sent the following e-mail to a few friends:

Shalom, my friends,

This is Belinda. How are you?

I'd like to share some good news with you. As many of you may know, I have been in a conversion process for a while. I'm glad to tell you that I have recently been granted approval by the Beis Din (the Jewish Court) for my conversion to Judaism.

I'll be going to the mikvah on Thursday to formally complete the conversion process. I'm very excited about it. I very much look forward to it, and my life thereafter. I want to share this joy with you.

Besides the studying and exam, I truly feel and experience the positive changes that Judaism brings to my life. It has been a significant and meaningful journey for me. Not to mention the very memorable and eye-opening trip to Israel in 1996.

I hope that you will be happy for me. I hope that everything goes well in all your dealings, with lots of opportunities for you to get the most "real pleasure" out of life.

Work hard to make a living and make time to do the living.

—Belinda (Bina Ester-to-be) ☺

The conversion happened exactly one year after I met the Beis Din for the first time. As it turned out, I needed to be on an Indian Reserve near Ottawa for some important job training, and had to miss the momentous event. Even after the assignment ended on Friday afternoon, I would not be able to leave for Toronto, as it would be too close to the onset of Shabbos. During Shabbos, which I spent with a very fine family in Ottawa, kindly arranged for me by my rabbi in Kingston, I decided to have some fun. Sometime during dinner, I cleared my throat and declared before my hosts and other guests present: "I have an announcement to make. I would like to share some wonderful news with you. As soon as Shabbos is over, I plan to drive to Toronto and propose marriage to a girl. Her name is *Bina Ester.* I have yet to meet her but we did speak by phone, and as far as I can tell, she is a very nice girl." I casually mentioned to my stunned audience that she was very pretty and exceptionally young—in fact, only two days old. Furthermore, I added, she was Chinese...

On Saturday night, I drove to Toronto and stayed overnight with Bina Ester's family. I was very curious to find out whether I could detect any difference in my girlfriend, now that she was Jewish. I was unable to. Physically, emotionally, intellectually, she was the same. Spiritually, I could not discern any changes, although I knew that she was fully, one hundred percent Jewish.

On Sunday afternoon we went for a walk and talked about her conversion experience. Her mother, sister, and a few good friends from the community had gone to the event. Lucy, from the Jerusalem Fellowship Program, attended too, and brought a "birthday" cake.

Belinda recounted that Leah, an Orthodox friend, escorted her to a small room that contained the mikvah. Belinda had specifically chosen Leah, with the Beis Din's approval, to be the one to ensure that the immersion would be valid. The mikvah was surrounded by white sheets, arranged in such a way that the three rabbis could see only the back of Belinda's head[35] from an adjacent office through the open doorway. The three men were otherwise very much present, and Belinda felt vulnerable as she stood stark naked in the water, her back to them, awaiting their instructions.

One of the rabbis, speaking in a deep, piercing voice that echoed in the tiny room, began to pose a string of questions in a heavy Eastern European accent. She felt as if God were speaking to her.

35. The Beis Din judges must be able to witness the head completely submerged in the water during the process of immersion.

Did she understand the consequences of her decision? Did she know what she was doing? Did she realize that she would henceforth be obligated in all the laws of the Torah, that she must eat only kosher food, that she must fast on Yom Kippur, et cetera, et cetera? Belinda was required to reply affirmatively to each question before the next one was posed. Belinda then dunked herself once, recited the two prescribed blessings, dunked herself two more times, and emerged from the water a Jew.

Following the immersion, Belinda joined friends and family who had been waiting upstairs, for a little *L'Hayyim* (toast to life) to mark her new commitment as a Jew. One of the rabbis performed the "baby-naming" ceremony, and Bina Ester received hugs and kisses and presents, including several books on Judaism.

Bina Ester told me that when she stepped out of the mikvah she felt "liberated" and "armed for life"—having inherited the tools necessary to fulfill her potential.

❧

In truth, I was very tempted to propose marriage as soon as I saw Bina Ester, but I had decided that I would give us at least a day to "get to know each other" as two Jews, before proposing lifelong commitment. Now that Belinda was Jewish, she could marry any Jewish bachelor she wanted, and it would only be fair, I reasoned, to give her the opportunity to experience — if only for a day — being an "unattached Jewish girl." It was probably more a formality than anything else. Besides, if I did *not* propose, would she have regretted, if only a little, that she converted?

On Sunday evening, we drove to Miami Grill, a kosher restaurant that served Chinese food. Before entering, I presented her a gift: a Star of David necklace, a present I had received for my Bar Mitzvah. The restaurant was crowded, and people were in earshot of each other's conversations. After ordering and filling our stomachs a little, I began to speak in a subdued voice about what I was looking for in a marriage, and in life in general. I reiterated my values, my aspirations, and my desire to be a good and faithful husband and what I thought that entailed. Then I took a sip of water, paused to take in the moment, and voiced the magic words in Cantonese — words with which I was thoroughly familiar, words I had repeated to myself a thousand times, words I prayed and dreamed so often of saying for the previous four years. *"Lei seung mseung tohn ngo geet fun?"* After a playful, teasingly long pause, Bina Ester responded, *"Avade"* (Yiddish for "Of course").

Chopsticks

More than a hundred guests filed into the large, elegant, Beth Avraham Yoseph of Toronto synagogue early on a Tuesday evening in March 1999. About forty percent were Chinese, consisting of Bina Ester's family and friends. From my side were my immediate family and several distant relatives. The rest were mutual friends, including a few rabbis. The wedding invitations were printed in English, Yiddish, and Chinese.

Adopting the custom of traditional Chinese weddings, everyone was invited to sign the "guest cloth"—a big, red, beautifully embroidered sheet of silk-like material that would later hang in our home.

Following the moving ceremony in the sanctuary, guests proceeded to the banquet hall, where they were treated to sumptuous Chinese as well as traditional Ashkenazi Jewish dishes. As an alternative to knife and fork, each guest was given a pair of souvenir chopsticks. On one chopstick was inscribed my name (in Hebrew and Chinese) and on the other Bina Ester's name (also in Hebrew and Chinese). The implicit message was that two "chopsticks" working together can accomplish considerably more than either chopstick by itself.

A special feature was a big-screen video presentation. It consisted of a sequence of photos, synchronized to upbeat music, of my ancestors in Europe and Bina Ester's ancestors in Hong Kong, down through the generations to the current newlywed couple.

The rabbi spoke eloquently. My father, two brothers, and a long-time family friend entertained everyone with music and song. There were heart-warming and amusing anecdotes from family and friends. "Bina Ester, we always knew you were Jewish," declared the master of ceremonies. "After all, you grew up eating Chinese food!" The bride and groom also made speeches. My wife opened with a few sentences in Yiddish, followed by English and Cantonese. I began with a few sentences of Cantonese and continued in Yiddish, English, and Italian.

The energy that evening ranged from very spirited to feverishly high. There were blessings, singing, and lively group dancing to Hebrew and Chinese music. The first song was "Hava Nagila" in Cantonese translation, to which Belinda had danced on a Hong Kong beach when she was a girl; she had no idea, then, that this was a popular Israeli Jewish song. The invitations had specified modest dress and no mixed (male/female) dancing, and this was wholly respected. In traditional Jewish weddings, the bride and groom are considered Queen and King. With this in mind, people danced exuberantly with us and around us, lifted us high up on chairs, juggled apples, knives, and torches, and performed other clown-like feats to entertain us. No professionals were hired. Friends brought their own props. Everyone joined in the merriment, even many of the Chinese guests for whom attending such an event was probably a real culture shock.

The event lasted until approximately 1:30 in the morning. Though a lot of the guests left early (they had to go to work the next morning), new faces appeared. These were mostly young and energetic members of Toronto's Jewish community who had learned about the wedding from Bina Ester's conversion teacher, and came to invigorate the dancing. They did not even know us personally. They came for the sole purpose of performing the mitzvah of bringing joy to the bride and groom on their wedding day.

After the wedding, we did not rush off on our honeymoon. As is the Jewish custom, seven days of celebration are held together with the community, during which the new couple continues to receive royal treatment. Each day, different friends and acquaintances arranged festive meals for us in their homes and invited at least ten other people to attend. We would be honoured at the head of the table, on the finest chairs, sometimes on cushions, and served regally. Blessings would be recited, good wishes extended. There was spontaneous singing, sometimes impromptu group dancing, and words of advice on building a happy and healthy marriage.

9

Ascribing Meaning

There is a Chinese saying that "anything with its back to the sky may be eaten by people." Belinda grew up eating exotic creatures that many Jews would find repulsive, such as squid, toad legs, and solidified pork blood. The occasional uninvited insects in vegetables were considered extra protein. Today she screams when she finds a bug in her salad — not because the insect is disgusting, but because it is not kosher!

Over the course of a few months I took the occasion of Shabbos and holiday invitations to ask my hosts the following hypothetical question: "Suppose someone were to convince you that the Torah is not of divine origin, how much, if any, of Jewish observance would you still keep?" The replies and ensuing discussions were interesting. One of my most religious friends said he would "drop the whole

193

thing." Upon cross-examination, however, he conceded that he would not harm people he disliked, or cheat on his taxes, and, in fact, he would abide by the vast majority of ethical laws and rules that are expected from citizens of Western society. Social conditioning and fear of legal repercussion were the main reasons. The ritual observances—such as keeping kosher or observing Shabbos—he would cease. Others responded that they would continue to keep most, if not all, the ritual observances in addition to the ethical laws because Judaism is a holistic discipline that provides needed structure to their lives and promotes psychological and emotional well-being.

Despite the range of responses, there is one point on which nearly everyone agreed: if the Torah is not the word of God, then there is no fundamental difference between a Jew and a non-Jew, and so there is no reason why one (or one's children) should not intermarry.

Most of the reasons Jewish people give themselves for not intermarrying are subjective. Some are products of a clannish mindset and border on racism; i.e., "We must not marry gentiles because they (or their culture, religion, et cetera) are different/inferior." Among other often heard arguments are, "It would kill my parents," "Because of the Holocaust," "Because of anti-Semitism," and "It threatens Jewish continuity." These reasons are tainted with guilt and prompt the question, Why be Jewish? What is so important about our heritage that we must sacrifice our happiness (refrain from marrying the person we love) for its sake? Many cultures exert pressure to marry one's own kind, but why give in to it—especially in a multicultural society?

There are no random events. My meeting Belinda was meant to be. Perhaps God knew that I needed someone from completely outside of Judaism to help me see my religion through objective eyes and appreciate its importance in a way that I couldn't otherwise. Moreover, the relationship forced me to look deeply into the labyrinth of Truth, and come face to face with a quintessential question of many religions: Did God author the Bible?

It's easier to believe that God exists than to believe He also gave us the Torah. I always believed in God, and many people who believe in God find nothing wrong with intermarriage. Believing that the Torah is of divine origin, on the other hand, has most significant implications for how our daily existence is to be consummated, and for our purpose in life.

Before I met Belinda, the question of how the Torah originated was of little interest to me. I knew I was Jewish; I had always felt Jewish, and, indeed, Judaism is much more than a religion. Judaism is culture and ethnicity. It is language and geography. It is a collective mindset forged by a particular set of historical experiences. One can quite easily live one's entire life as a Jew guided by these influences. But, if one were to strip away these layers, one would discover, as I did, the core essence of Judaism: an elixir that has kept a particular people united for 3,300 years. While Jewish culture, Jewish languages, Jewish geography, and Jewish mindset have evolved and changed, the Torah has remained unchanged. If there is one factor that is of ultimate value, infinitely profound, and *uniquely* Jewish, it is the Torah. It is the one ingredient without which Judaism could easily, in a matter of a few generations, become unrecognizably transformed or diluted, and eventually vanish in the sea of competing social norms.

It is against the backdrop of acquiring greater appreciation of the richness of my Jewish heritage, understanding the indispensability of the Torah in preserving it, and realizing that the Torah prohibits a Jew from marrying a gentile, that I struggled long and hard with the question of whether to continue dating my Chinese girlfriend. In the end, the prospect that God Himself authored the Torah raised the stakes to a non-negotiable level.

Prescribed Role

As it was, Belinda and I eventually came to the conclusion (in her case, with more certainty) that the Torah is of divine origin and that the interpretations given by the Orthodox rabbis are true, or at least the closest thing to the Truth that we know. Following this premise, there are *prescribed roles* for Jewish people and for non-Jewish people. That such a proposition may seem inappropriate in our present-day culture of political correctness is immaterial. The conclusion follows from the premise; if the premise is true, so must the conclusion be true. "Logical correctness" supersedes political correctness.[36]

---

36. That there are different roles does not imply that one role is superior to the other. Superiority and inferiority are notions that stem from a paradigm of competitiveness. In our attempt to improve the state of the world, we are all in the same boat.

A Jew's prescribed role is to live the Torah way of life and, in doing so, to be an ethical role model to other Jews and to the rest of humanity. This is not to say that Jews are more ethical in their behaviour than gentiles, only that they have a broader (and highly detailed) set of responsibilities in this domain, as reflected in the greater number of mitzvos they were given.

If the Orthodox view is correct, a Jew has no choice in this matter. She can try to convert out of Judaism, but in the eyes of the Torah and God she remains a Jew (albeit an apostate one). Once a Jew, she is a Jew forever. She cannot escape her destiny. She can shirk her assigned responsibilities, fill her life with distractions, convince herself that she is no different from a gentile, but ultimately a Jewish soul will leave her body when she dies.

A man and a woman look different and have inherently different roles. A dog, a star, and a flower each have different purposes in the world, reflecting their different characteristics. But there is no physical difference between a Jew and a non-Jew. Bina Ester looks exactly the same as Belinda did. Her emotional, intellectual, and psychological makeup immediately before and after her immersion in the mikvah was identical. Her new role as a Jew was unaccompanied by any corresponding change, however small, in her external self. Why is that?

God assigns roles (purposes) and endows the custodians of these roles with appropriate attributes. A dog and a star and a flower have different characteristics *because* they have different functions. One can postulate that the reason Jews and non-Jews do not necessarily appear different is that their role as moral teachers and role models do not require any unique physical features. Moreover, any person may become Jewish if he or she is sincerely committed. Were some physical change to miraculously occur whenever a person converted, there would be a loss of free will in fulfilling the new responsibilities, because of the obviousness of God's expectations.

Granted, the notion of a prescribed role for the Jewish people is very difficult to accept, in that the soul is intangible. How can my Chinese wife have the same "role" in the world as an African-American Jew or a Spanish Jew or an Arab Jew, while having a considerably different role from a billion Chinese people? It seems counter-intuitive. Be that as it may, many secular Jews have not investigated the matter, despite the immense personal ramifications of a Jew-Gentile role dichotomy.

The consequences of not investigating are significant. We Jews tend to be ambivalent and confused about our identity. We are in various states of spiritual angst, groping for meaning, sometimes in extreme places. Our innate drive to "repair the world" (tikkun olam) is reflected in our being disproportionately represented in cults and the Eastern religions. Although small in number, we occupy prominent positions in social and political movements, in some cases healthy ones, in other cases not.

The point here is not to extol the influence and power of Jews. It is to underscore the possibility that the overwhelming majority of us are, because of our ignorance of the Torah, not fulfilling our prescribed role.

All-or-Nothing?

Studies indicate that the rate of intermarriage among Jews in North America has risen dramatically over the past few decades. Currently, it is around fifty percent.

Though such statistics are ominous, it is important to recognize that intermarriage, like interdating, is a *symptom* rather than the root of a problem. In the favourable context of a free society, lessened anti-Semitism, and shared values of human decency, intermarriage is the natural consequence of religious ignorance and assimilation.

A widespread belief that discourages unaffiliated Jews from investigating their spiritual heritage is that practising Orthodox Judaism is "all-or-nothing." This mindset is unfortunate. Judaism is a process, a journey to a more fulfilling life. Every small step is a significant accomplishment in and of itself. Each mitzvah that we perform strengthens our relationship with the Creator in some unique way, and is of infinite value. The all-or-nothing principle is untenable: If you are unable to acquire a pot full of gold coins, isn't having a small part of it better than having none at all?

My parents, although not Orthodox in the full ritualistic sense, nevertheless exemplify strong Jewish values in many areas. Honouring elders, visiting the sick and bereaved, demonstrating family loyalty, extending hospitality to guests, and giving utmost dedication to the moral upbringing of their children, are among the basic Torah mitzvos at which they excel. Thanks to the many years of Jewish education and experiences to which they exposed me, I was able to hang on to my religious heritage, if, at times, only by a thread.

No one can do it all. Judaism addresses every facet of life. Given life's complexity and the imperfect human condition, it is rare for someone to attain total mastery.

It appears that a gentile wishing to become Jewish is at an unfair disadvantage: she must commit herself totally to the dictates of the Torah, whereas someone born Jewish has the "luxury" of committing herself to less. A key to unravelling this perplexity is this: the all-or-nothing notion is indeed invalid — but only if one is growth-oriented. Otherwise it can be used as an excuse for minimal observance.

A gentile, unlike a Jew, is not obligated to follow Jewish law; she is not even obligated to become Jewish. The rabbinical courts have a very heavy responsibility to ensure that only sincere and committed gentiles gain membership in the "club," for once someone joins, she can never leave, and she is forever accountable to God and the Jewish people for her commitment and observances.

צ֑

This book speaks to the potential for Jewish growth through dating a gentile. To suggest that I could not have come to discover the beauty of Torah except through interdating would be overstating the case. But to propose that my relationship with Belinda was not an opportune blessing in terms of igniting and fanning the flames of my Jewish growth would be equally untrue.

This blessing was bestowed upon me neither accidentally nor as a *fait accompli*. In fact, in countless other cases, such a "blessing" is really a tribulation, leading to intermarriage, confused loyalties, strained or damaged relationships, and, possibly, years of spiritual anguish and suffering.

When I met Belinda, I was already relatively well educated in many aspects of Judaism, with the notable exception of God and Torah. It is these confounding areas of Judaism that are most replete with misconceptions and prejudices. And it is precisely in these matters, which demand the most intense scrutiny, that my persistent questioning made the crucial difference in transforming my lifestyle from secular to Torah-observant.

Belinda was an important catalyst in the process. For instance, whereas I might otherwise be indifferent about seeking clarification on a minor point that did not make sense in a lecture, I dared not be complacent if it was a matter that bothered *her*. It was so important to me that my girlfriend find Judaism a logically satisfying and beautiful system that, during the years that we dated, I ran to rabbis or researched on my own any issues that crept up, however trivial the issues may have seemed. I only wish I can continue to sustain this level of fervour now that Belinda is Jewish and we are married.

To be a serious Jew — whether observant or not — requires serious questioning. Judaism can demonstrate its validity and relevance to us only if we investigate and challenge it.

Timeless Treasure

In my childhood, God was an old man with a white beard, gazing down from his crimson throne on top of snow-white clouds, meting out punishments to people who did bad things and rewards to people who did good things. Thirty years later, my image of God, while no longer anthropomorphic, is not much more sophisticated. However, my image of *myself* has changed considerably: I am more humble and aware of how simplistic my perception of God continues to be — including my perception of what He wants of us.

I believe there is much, much more to God, Torah, and Judaism than I have been exposed to through my learning. I don't understand why only one nation chose to receive the Torah (and hence, become the "Chosen People") and why all other nations rejected this tremendous privilege and responsibility. I don't fully understand how rabbis can be so certain that the Torah could not have been authored by people. I don't understand in what way and to what extent God gets upset each time a Jew flicks a light switch on Friday night.

But I know that life is short, and I will never have all the answers that I seek; I will only increase my number of questions. At least, I hope such will be the case. In the meantime, I choose to live as if God is real, as if the Torah is true, for that makes more sense to me than living as if

God does not exist, and as if the Torah is not the Truth; and certainly it makes more sense to me than many of the values and practices espoused by secular society.

It's easy to question and therefore not do. Some in the Orthodox world choose to do and not to question. I choose to do, while at the same time to question, learn, and grow.

I am glad I did not heed Rabbi Silver's advice when he urged me to end my relationship with Belinda shortly after I had met her. I have had other off-putting interactions with Orthodox rabbis, from which I tried as much as possible to shelter Belinda. They have been relatively few and far between. I believe that experiences should be put in perspective. Still, lessons learned from any single experience are timeless; they do not expire when more positive experiences come along. To this day, I continue to seek out rabbis' advice when I need to lean on their knowledge and insight to properly investigate an issue. Judaism, I strongly believe, is about questioning and self-education, not blindly following rabbis. I consider myself as independent a thinker as when I was secular.

While writing this final chapter, I asked my wife whether she had any message for her fellow Jews. She replied as follows: "As an outsider, I had to knock very hard and persistently at the door to get access to the Torah, a timeless treasure that is given to you by the Creator of this world. Isn't it worth taking some time to check out this treasure that has been sitting all this time in your own backyard?"

I myself came to discover this treasure in my backyard, but it required seeing it through foreign eyes. One evening, seated at my Shabbos table with Belinda, I melted into tears: for years I had sought the formula for world peace. For years I discovered compelling logic and simple beauty in one human-made "ism" after another, but in each case I would sooner or later uncover some underlying flaw. In the case of Judaism, by contrast, the deeper I dug, the more the system made sense. Human nature is incredibly complex; no simple, intuitive prescription for living will do. If only I had realized this principle years ago! Moreover, while all religions may preach basic moral values such as peace and brotherly love, they are not necessarily equally effective in transmitting these values and translating them into specific behaviours and actions.

The impulse to investigate a religion does not always derive from a cool, rational agenda. Often it comes from a favourable impression one forms of its practitioners. Notwithstanding Rabbi Silver's wise counsel, "Do not judge Judaism by the Jews," a healthy Jewish environment is conducive to motivating secular Jews to look into Judaism. In many locales, Judaism is stagnant and stale. Its rituals are performed perfunctorily and without an ounce of passion; its lifecycle events are tedious; its worship services mind-numbing; its congregations dormant or arrogant; its celebrations formal and lifeless. Living Jewishly can be little more than an excuse for materialistic indulgence (the lavish but spiritually skimpy Bar Mitzvah parties, for instance) or a way to appease feelings of guilt. It is easy to be turned off by it all. On the other hand, one will find numerous communities — Reform to Orthodox — where Jewish life is growth-oriented and vibrant, imbued with freshness and spirituality. Here Judaism may be intellectual or it may be mystical, but it is humbling and burning with passion.

With increasing globalization, career changes, geographic mobility, and social and technological transformation, it is ever easier to lose clarity over one's purpose and direction in life. In our times, many people do not feel attached to a community, are isolated from family, and have no sense of who they are. There is a growing body of Jews who feel a void in their lives, and search far and wide for answers and deeper meaning. Many find a niche in other religions only to return months or years later to Judaism through the hand of Providence. Others remain permanently entrenched in the foreign belief system, never knowing that many of the same spiritual treasures that attracted them to these religions could be found in their own heritage, if they took the time to investigate properly.

Western society is constantly challenging previously held values, and there is a sense that we are drifting without a moral anchor. Cults continue to attract a lot of young (and not so young) individuals, as they tend to offer more immediate rewards and heightened sense of purpose than do main-stream religions. If one is fortunate to resist this temptation and avoid the harmful side effects of cults, one is still faced with a plethora of religions, as well as cultures and lifestyles, from which to choose. Consider this scenario: a woman who "found" Buddhism while attending university has a Catholic mother and a Jewish father. After graduating and landing a job, she meets and falls in love with a co-worker — a Muslim immigrant from Iran. How are they to raise their children?

What language, what culture, which rituals, and which beliefs?

Bina Ester and I are attempting to raise our children with as much of our ethnic languages and cultures as we can, to instil in them a sense of connectedness to their roots and heritage. At the same time, we recognize that languages and cultures are never static, and the environment in which we live out our lives is constantly changing. Ideally, one would try to get hold of some deeper anchor that has proven resilient to different climates and can withstand the pressures of changing times. For us, this anchor is the Torah, a 3,300-year-old system that has survived in the most diverse and hostile environments and which Bina Ester and I believe is the way that God intends for Jews to live.

Judaism is a beautiful and meaningful religion for anyone who chooses it. As my wife said to me, "If I knew about the tension and frustration that would develop in our relationship because of your religion before we started dating, I would have chosen not to date you *at all*. But if I also understood what the Torah was about, the quality of family life and personal growth that it could lead to, I would undoubtedly do it all over again."

Undoubtedly, so would I.

Afterword

by Bina Ester Botwinik

At the time of this book's publication, my husband and I are living in Ottawa, Canada, with our two young children.

Being a Torah-observant Jew was an inconceivable option for me when I was growing up. I am tremendously grateful to God for having drawn me into the "club." The Orthodox Jewish way of life is permeated with potential for meaningful happiness and continual self-improvement. Through learning Torah, I have increased my awareness of the Omnipresent, developed greater sensitivity to people, and acquired a healthier attitude toward life. When I was born, my mother named me *Hang-Yee*, which means "the fortunate one." I feel extremely fortunate to have discovered this great manual of "Instructions for Living" and to continue to experience positive changes in myself.

When I met Yankl, I knew nothing about Judaism or the possible challenges that I might face by dating a Jew. I am thankful that it turned out to be a rewarding and memorable journey, although it was also the most stressful and frustrating experience of my life. Emotionally, I was at a dead end, hitting my head against a brick wall, all the while fearing the imminent termination of a magnificent relationship and possibly mourning the loss of someone close. Yankl and I were so much together, and yet we could not *be* together. It was very painful.

I am convinced that Jews who choose to date gentiles bear a responsibility to figure out what Judaism will mean for them as life unfolds. It is imperative to make an informed decision whether or not one will honour one's heritage when significant life-cycle events (marriage, circumcision, holidays, Bar Mitzvah, and so on) take place, before deciding whom to date. Many Jews wake up to their strong need to follow the traditions of their ancestors when it is already too late to prevent deep emotional hurt to their innocent gentile partner. This is irresponsible.

A few of my Chinese relatives and secular Jewish friends are baffled by my decision to lead a Torah-observant lifestyle, which, from their perspective, entails tremendous inconveniences. Isn't life complicated and demanding enough as it is?

My husband and I recently bought a digital camcorder. We were able to invoke many functions through the self-explanatory control buttons: record, rewind, play, et cetera. I read the user's manual, just to see what else this tiny metal box could do. "What a great machine!" I discovered. "Amazing capabilities!" I felt I got my money's worth and I remember thinking that the next version of this contraption would probably cook my supper! There was so much more than just recording and playing. Even after having read the booklet, I still could not remember many of the available functions. However, I knew that I could always refer to the manual, thereby capitalizing on my investment and deriving maximum enjoyment.

This is how I feel about our precious Torah, and the world in which God places us. We can easily go through life without His instructions. We won't know what we are missing until we take the time to investigate.

**Want to share your thoughts about this book?
Please turn to page 215.**

╓ People of the Book?

Did you know that while the Jews are called "the people of the Book", it was the Chinese who invented paper and printing? According to tradition, paper was invented by Cai Lun, an official of the Emporer He Di, in the year 105 A.D. And printing was invented well over a thousand years ago in the Far East, almost certainly in China.

Source: Karen Brookfield, *Book* (Dorling Kindersley Ltd, 1993)

Glossary

Ashkenazi
> Descendant from European Jews, historically Yiddish-speaking, who settled in eastern, central, and northern Europe.

Bar Mitzvah
> A public ceremony held around a Jewish boy's thirteenth birthday (technically, his entry into his fourteenth year) to mark the fact that he is henceforth obligated in all Torah observances.

Beis Din (or Bet Din)
> Rabbinical court.

berakhah
> Blessing.

Hagaddah
> A basic text used to recount the story of the Exodus.

Kiddush
> Shabbos prayer chanted over wine (or grape juice).

kippa
> A small, usually round, head covering typically worn by observant Jewish males.

latkes
> Potato pancakes that Ashkenazi Jews customarily eat during the holiday of Hanukkah. Jews of Spanish or

North African descent tend to eat *sufganiyot* (doughnuts) instead.

mezuzah

Small capsule containing several passages of the Torah, including one referring to the Oneness of God, that is placed on doorposts of Jewish homes and buildings in accordance with the biblical commandment.

menorah

A candelabrum having seven branches as used in the Temple in Jerusalem in Biblical times. The word "menorah" is also used (by Ashkenazi Jews) to refer to a nine-branch candelabrum used during the festival of Hanukkah.

mikvah

Ritual body of water.

mitzvah

Biblical commandment. The plural form is *mitzvos*.

rebbe

Teacher.

Seder

Festive reliving of the Exodus from Egypt, conducted during the spring holiday of Passover.

Shabbos

Also known as the Sabbath or Shabbat.

shlep

Traipse or trudge.

shtetl

A small Eastern European town.

siddur

Jewish prayer book.

Sukkos (or Sukkot)

A seven-day festival, beginning on the fifteenth day of the seventh Jewish lunar month, in which Jews dwell in temporary huts of specified dimension and construction (See Leviticus 23:34—43).

tefillin

Two small, black leather cubes with leather straps, containing parchments inscribed with certain Torah verses. One is strapped onto the left arm (generally) and the other onto the forehead and worn during prayer services.

Torah

The Hebrew Bible. Literally, it means "instructions" or "teaching."

yeshiva

Jewish religious school.

Yom Kippur

Day of Atonement.

Upcoming Titles
from Paper Spider

How to Screen Your Dates
Secret shortcuts to a successful relationship

Anything is Possible
Overcoming challenges to Jewish observance

The *Touch* Factor
Getting in touch with the real purpose of sexuality

Share Your Thoughts

Feel free to share your thoughts about this book by posting your comments on these web sites:

www.PaperSpider.Net
www.Amazon.com

or by filling out the form on the next page.

We may share your input with others by placing it in newspapers, or other print or electronic media.

Don't know where to start? These questions may be helpful:

1. *What* do you especially like or dislike about the book's content?

2. *Why?* Please give details.

3. *How* did reading this book affect your awareness or views about the subject matter of the book?

Fax or mail your comments to us
Fax: 613-321-9866

Name	
Profession (& Title)	
City & Country	
Email address	
Phone number	

Submissions become property of Paper Spider and may be used for publicity.

Your comments

Tear

·························· Fold top ⤸ Tape or glue to the bottom ··························

Paper Spider, Readers' Reviews

Suite 8, 1821 Walkley Road,
Room B101, Ottawa,
Ontario, K1H 6X9
Canada

············· Fold here ⤦ to expose address above for postal mail ·············

Fax or mail your comments to us
Fax: 613-321-9866

Name	
Profession (& Title)	
City & Country	
Email address	
Phone number	

Submissions become property of Paper Spider and may be used for publicity.

Your comments

Tear

Paper Spider, Readers' Reviews

Suite 8, 1821 Walkley Road,
Room B101, Ottawa,
Ontario, K1H 6X9
Canada

Get more copies

Toll free 1-888-BOOKS-88 (1-888-266-5788)

Phone direct 613-321-9850

www.PaperSpider.Net

This book makes a great gift!
No matter whether you want to get a copy
for yourself, or for family and friends, you can
easily order by phone, fax, postal mail or via the Internet.

See next page for order form.

Order Form

Chicken Soup with Chopsticks	Qty.	Subtotal (US$)
Soft cover ISBN 0-9732523-1-6 **US$18.18**		
Hard cover ISBN 0-9732523-0-8 **US$22.18**		
Shipping & handling (FIRST item) $ 4.95 to U.S. & Canada $28.00 to other countries		
Add $2 for each item after the FIRST item to US & Canada; or $10 to other countries		
Sales Tax (Canadian provinces only) 7% for AB, BC, MB, NT, NU, ON, PE, QC, SK, YT 15% for NB, NF, NS		
Total in US$		

Purchaser Information		
Full Name		
☐ Credit Card number	(VISA or Master Card ONLY)	
Signature		(Exp. mm/yyyy)
☐ Payment enclosed	US$ or (multiply by 1.3) CAN$ (Canadian cheques, US cheques or money orders ONLY)	
Email Address		
Daytime Phone no.		
Street Address		
City, Province/State		
Postal Code/ZIP		
Country		

Fax your order to: **613-321-9866**

or mail it to: **Paper Spider, Book Order**
Suite 8, 1821 Walkley Road
Room B101, Ottawa
ON, K1H 6X9 Canada

Tear

www.PaperSpider.Net
Phone 1-888-BOOKS-88

Order Form

Chicken Soup with Chopsticks	Qty.	Subtotal (US$)
Soft cover ISBN 0-9732523-1-6 **US$18.18**		
Hard cover ISBN 0-9732523-0-8 **US$22.18**		
Shipping & handling (FIRST item) $ 4.95 to U.S. & Canada $28.00 to other countries		
Add $2 for each item after the FIRST item to US & Canada; or $10 to other countries		
Sales Tax (Canadian provinces only) 7% for AB, BC, MB, NT, NU, ON, PE, QC, SK, YT 15% for NB, NF, NS		
Total in US$		

Purchaser Information		
Full Name		
☐	Credit Card number	(VISA or Master Card ONLY)	
	Signature		(Exp. mm/yyyy)
☐	Payment enclosed	US$　　　　or (multiply by 1.3) CAN$ (Canadian cheques, US cheques or money orders ONLY)	
Email Address		
Daytime Phone no.		
Street Address		
City, Province/State		
Postal Code/ZIP		
Country		

Fax your order to: **613-321-9866**

or mail it to: **Paper Spider, Book Order**
Suite 8, 1821 Walkley Road
Room B101, Ottawa
ON, K1H 6X9 Canada

Paper Spider

www.PaperSpider.Net
Phone 1-888-BOOKS-88

Printed in the United States
43526LVS00005B/199